The Debater's Guide

Southern Illinois University Press
Carbondale and Edwardsville

The Debater's Guide

Revised Edition

Jon M. Ericson &
James J. Murphy

with Raymond Bud Zeuschner

To Don, Barrie, Edie, Mike, Dan, Bob, Denise, Lynette, Rich, Chris, Robin . . . and all student debaters learning to think critically and to articulate clearly.

Copyright © 1987 by the Board of Trustees
Southern Illinois University
All rights reserved
Printed in the United States of America
Edited by Sarah Mitchell
Designed by Cindy Small
Production supervised by Natalia Nadraga

Library of Congress Cataloging-in-Publication Data

Ericson, Jon M.
  The debater's guide.
  Bibliography: p.
  1. Debates and debating.   I. Murphy, James Jerome.   II. Zeuschner,
Raymond F.   III. Title.
PN4181.E65   1987   808.53   86-33855
ISBN 0-8093-1386-3

02 01 00 99   6 5 4 3

Contents

The Debater's Guide

There are only two parts to a speech:
You make a statement and you prove it.

—Aristotle, *Rhetoric*

1

The Value of Debate

Debate is one of the oldest activities of civilization. Calm, orderly *debate,* in which speakers argue for acceptance of various answers to a given question, is an obvious feature of modern parliaments and congresses. But it also had its place in the deliberations of ancient kings, who maintained councils of nobles to give them advice. When the nobles disagreed, they were allowed to debate their proposals before the king, who acted as the final judge in choosing one plan of action.

In modern democratic societies, the right to debate is a priceless asset. It enables any citizen to propose a better plan of action than the one which the ruling power sets forth. If the speaker can convince enough citizens that the new idea is a better one, then the speaker can literally change the policy of the city, county, state, or even nation.

In the United States, there are various ways in which the effective speaker can propose a new solution to a problem. One way, for instance, is to persuade a number of people to sign a petition to put a proposal on the ballot in an election. Then the proponents can speak to the voters on behalf of the proposal and perhaps convince a sufficient number of them to vote it into law. They will undoubtedly meet outspoken opposition if they attempt to use this method of expressing their opinions, and it is essential that they know what to do in this kind of debating situation. By the same token, a good speaker can defend the present system, or status quo, by opposing unsound ideas.

We are accustomed to the formal debating done by members of legislative bodies such as the Senate or House of Representatives. In these houses, elaborate rules are laid out to ensure adherence to the two basic rules of debate:

1. Present one issue at a time.
2. Provide equal opportunity for presentation of each point of view.

The committee system in the United States Congress, for example, makes it possible to begin debate on a bill even before it reaches the floor. But whether it is debated in a committee hearing (with the committee as judges) or on the floor of one of the two houses, the same basic principles are involved.

You may not be particularly conscious of the fact that debate occurs in many aspects of life, not only in congresses. Actually, every situation which asks you to compare alternatives is a situation forcing you to debate the merits of those alternatives. Sometimes you will do the debating within yourself, as when you must decide whether to attend college. Sometimes the debating is done in your presence by others, with you as the judge, as in the case of rival sales representatives, each of whom asks you to buy his or her particular product. Often, we fail to recognize the debate situation because there is only one person speaking to us—the single salesperson in a store, for instance—but usually that person reveals the true nature of the debate by acting as if there were actually a third person present with you. Such phrases as "You may be thinking that this would be expensive, but . . ." are signs of an awareness on the sellers' part that they must refute arguments which can be brought against their proposal by one part of your self so that the judging part of your self will decide in their favor. Therefore, the debating you do now can be a great help to you all your life. And you do not have to be a lawyer or member of Congress to use debating skills.

What are the advantages of debate for you? Since the first formal intercollegiate debate in 1892 (between Harvard and Yale) hundreds of thousands, perhaps even millions, of American high-school and college students have participated in academic debate. Woodrow Wilson engaged in debating as a student at Princeton long before becoming president of that university, governor of his state, and finally president of the United States. Presidents Kennedy, Nixon, Johnson, and Carter are other examples of national figures who participated in debating as students.

But you can spend four, or even eight, school years in debating and come out with little benefit unless you know what it is you are trying to do and what it is you are trying to learn. *The Debater's Guide* is dedicated to two closely related ideas: first, that you cannot do a job well unless you know what the job is; and second, that you can never fully understand the job unless you are able to do it well. Therefore, as you will find, debate's advantages for you coincide exactly with the qualities which are the virtues of an ideal debater:

1. Ability to collect and organize ideas. A successful debate speaker is one who can absorb vast amounts of material and select from it those items which are the best to use in a particular debate.

2. Ability to subordinate ideas. A debater will hear about forty-five hundred to five thousand words from the opponents during a typical single round of debate. Together with a colleague, this debater will deliver an additional forty-five hundred to five thousand words. Only by sorting out the major ideas from the minor ones can any speaker hope to make sense from this flood of words.

3. Ability to evaluate evidence. Skill in selecting out the really important evidence is a hallmark of an intelligent speaker. Not every statement, quotation, statistic, or idea in a debate is worth the trouble of refutation.

4. Ability to see logical connections. Aristotle once pointed out that the ability to see what is similar among dissimilar things is a mark of genius. The great mass of data presented during

most debates causes confusion among the hearers. Therefore, the speakers who can identify the relationship between items help to clarify the debate for the audience and thus improve their own chances for success.

5. Ability to think and speak in outline terms. Clarity is essential in a debate (and any good communication for that matter) where the clash of ideas often confuses an audience. The debaters must not only have a perfectly clear mental outline of their entire case, but they must also be able to communicate the sense of that outline to the audience.

6. Ability to speak convincingly. An awareness of what an audience expects—what it takes to convince that particular audience—is absolutely essential, both in debate and in other types of speaking.

7. Ability to adapt. Since a debate is a fluid situation, constantly changing as new ideas are introduced by various speakers, it places a premium on readiness of reply. In practice, this readiness means that you must not only be well-organized, logical, analytic, and convincing but also that you must react to new ideas quickly.

These are the skills which *The Debater's Guide* hopes to make easier for you to develop. They will be valuable to you not only in your school debating but also in every choice you make throughout your life, because every genuine choice involves a genuine debate. And in the larger context of the democratic society in which you live, your ability to present your point of view may be even more important, both to your own interest and to the interests of preserving and protecting that democratic society. As Adlai Stevenson has said: "I would remind you of an axiom in political science: people get the kind of government they deserve. Your public servants serve you right. Our American government may be defined, perhaps, as the government that really cares about the people. Just so, our government demands, it depends upon the care and devotion of the people" (R. Keith Kane, ed., "The Educated Citizen." In *What I Think* [New York: Harper and Brothers, 1956]).

Debate skill cannot by itself make good citizens, but the American who cannot speak effectively in an organized way is a voiceless citizen, one whose good ideas may be lost in the crowd or never heard. Debating, consequently, can be highly valuable both to you and to your society.

2

Understanding the Debate Process

The Debate Proposition

Almost every topic for school debate is a proposition of value or a proposition of policy. That is, they are statements asserting the value or worth of something or asserting that some course of action should be followed—some new policy should be adopted. For instance, here are some national debate topics of past years:

Value-Oriented Propositions:

1. Resolved: That education has failed its mission in the United States.

2. Resolved: That Affirmative Action promotes deleterious hiring practices.

3. Resolved: That a United States foreign policy significantly directed towards the furtherance of human rights is desirable.

4. Resolved: That the individual rights of privacy are more important than any other Constitutional right.

5. Resolved: That the United States is justified in aiding undemocratic governments.

Policy Propositions:

1. Resolved: That all United States military intervention

into the internal affairs of any foreign nation or nations in the Western Hemisphere should be prohibited.

2. Resolved: That the federal government should significantly curtail the powers of labor unions in the United States.

3. Resolved: That the United States should significantly increase its foreign military commitments.

4. Resolved: That the federal government should significantly strengthen the regulation of mass media communication in the United States.

Speakers who wish to debate must first understand what they are trying to do when they agree to defend or oppose one of these statements. What is a value-oriented proposition? What is a policy proposition? What happens in a debate? We can best begin to answer these questions with a look at the various topics.

In value-oriented topics, three elements are found:

1. The item being evaluated or about which the value judgment(s) is (are) being made. Usually, this item is the subject of the sentence. For example, "Resolved: That free trade is desirable."

2. The verb, which tells you which of the three tenses the topic deals with. The topic can use the historical evaluation in the past tense ("General Custer was unjustified in his battle strategy."). Or a generalized statement can be used ("Freedom of speech is the most important Constitutional right."). Or the topic can be speculative in the future tense ("Offshore oil development will be harmful."). In school debate, the generalized present tense *is* has been the most commonly used verb.

3. The term doing the evaluation—for example, *harmful* or *beneficial* or *deleterious*. A more complete discussion of these items will come in chapter 5.

In policy propositions, each topic contains certain key elements as well, although they have slightly different functions from the comparable elements of value-oriented propositions. The elements found are:

1. An agent to do the acting—for example, "The United States should adopt a policy of free trade." Again, it is the subject of the sentence.

2. The verb *should*—in other words, the first part of a verb urging an action.

3. An action verb to follow the *should* verb. For example, *should adopt* meaning to put a program or policy into action through governmental means.

4. A specification of direction or a limitation of the action desired. The phrase *free trade*, for example, gives direction and limits to the topic which would in this case eliminate consideration of increasing tariffs, discussing diplomatic recognition, or discussing interstate commerce.

The Proposition of Fact

Another kind of debate topic, which is almost never used in school debating, is called a *proposition of fact*. An example is, "The cause of the mid-air collision was a faulty radio receiver," or "The defendant is guilty of murder." The proposition of fact asks for proof of the previous existence of a fact. It is always marked by a linking verb—such as *is* or *was*. The only matter to be settled is whether a thing or state already exists. Consequently, the proposition of fact always deals with the past: what caused a collision which has already occurred; who killed a person already dead? Even a proposition like, "The Empire State Building is 831 feet tall" deals with a past fact, since the building must have existed before the asking of that question. This time element is extremely important because it limits such a debate to a yes-or-no reply. Because of this limitation, propositions of fact are seldom used for interschool debate, although they are almost exclusively the type found in the courtroom. They impose severe restrictions upon the amount of evidence which can be gathered, as well as upon the proposal of alternative solutions.

The Proposition of Value

Propositions of value aim to establish the worth of something. The difficulty involved in this type of proposition is that you must find acceptable proofs for assertions which may seem very subjective in nature. Criteria must be established by the affirmative which applies to the evaluation. For example, what constitutes desirable? When do we reach the level of positive associations so that we move into the area called desirable? Thus the debate is often in two major parts: (1) the quality or reasonableness of the evaluating term; and (2) the application of that term to the subject term of the sentence. Additional areas for case development, as well as refinements of these two elements, will come in chapter 5.

The Proposition of Policy

Propositions of policy deal with future action. Nothing has yet occurred. The entire debate is about whether something ought to occur. What you agree to do when you accept the affirmative side in such a debate is to offer sufficient and compelling reasons for an audience to perform the future action which you propose. When you agree to accept the negative side, you actually enter into a contract to offer sufficient reasons for an audience to reject the affirmative's arguments.

Ground Rules For American Debating

It should be clear at this point that the very nature of the debate encounter leads to certain ground rules, or general principles. The first of these principles is that the *affirmative side* agrees to support the proposition while the *negative side* agrees to counter that effort. More will be said about that agreement in a later chapter, but before leaving the matter of the debate proposition it might be useful to look briefly at a further aspect of the debate itself.

When you agree to defend one approach to the debate proposition—whether the negative or affirmative side—you also obligate yourself, in American debate practice, to use only that single approach required by the terms of the debate. In other words, you agree to act as an advocate of only one point of view. This practice is contrary to British school debating, or so-called parliamentary debate, in which a speaker usually can choose any point of view, can adapt that viewpoint to other speakers as the debate progresses, and can even reverse argument and join forces with the opposition if desired. A debate topic in the Oxford Union is often phrased as a question or as a general expression of attitude: "Resolved: That the House deplores the South African situation"; or "Is there a solution to the South African crisis?" Many sides will thus be possible in such a debate format.

American debating, on the other hand, involves matching two sets of advocates who have agreed to maintain consistently opposed points of view. This system is followed, literally, for the sake of argument. Such a contract with the opposing speakers and with the audience is entered into so that both affirmative and negative arguments may receive the undivided attention of one pair of debaters. From the standpoint of the audience, this procedure makes for efficiency of discussion—each side trying to present every available bit of evidence and reasoning in the best possible light. Each speaker benefits in two ways: first, by giving undivided attention to one approach to the problem; and second, by being required to reply to another speaker or speakers who have given equal thought to their specific approach.

The Debate Procedure

Sequence of Speeches

The standard American procedure calls for what is known as *university style debate*. In this system, two persons form a team and usually debate both affirmative and negative sides during a tournament. The affirmative begins the debate by presenting a *constructive*, the first affirmative speech, which makes a case for adopting the resolution. The next speaker is the first negative, who is followed by the second affirmative, and finally, the second negative. Most tournaments also include cross-examination periods between each constructive speech. Without the cross-examination the format is often termed *Oxford debate*. With the cross-examination periods it is simply termed *cross-examination debate* or sometimes *Oregon style*. After a short pause, which is often omitted, the second negative constructive speaker is followed by the first negative rebuttal speaker. In the *rebuttal* speech, the speaker may attack the opponents' arguments in addition to defense, but may not introduce any new constructive arguments. The speakers then continue to alternate again with first affirmative rebuttal, second negative rebuttal, and finally, second affirmative rebuttal. Including cross-examinations, the sequence is as follows:

Constructive Speeches:
First Affirmative
    Cross-Examination by Second Negative
First Negative
    Cross-Examination by First Affirmative
Second Affirmative
    Cross-Examination by First Negative
Second Negative
    Cross-Examination by Second Affirmative
Rebuttal Speeches:
First Negative
First Affirmative
Second Negative
Second Affirmative

It should be noted that the negative side has the last speech in the constructive series, while the affirmative has the last speech in the rebuttal series. This sequence equalizes the opportunity of reply, since the last speaker in a series has an advantage in this respect.

Time Limits

American high schools and colleges both usually use eight minutes for constructive speeches, three minutes for cross-examinations, and four minutes for rebuttals. In the Oxford style, high schools usually keep the 8-4 format, while colleges often shift to a 10-5 format. It is not unusual to find college cross-examination formats which are 8-3-5 as well as 10-3-5. Most time limits are a matter of custom and may be set by individual tournament hosts or association rules. There are even formats for one-person teams (called *Lincoln-Douglas style*) which vary in their time allotments. No matter which time format is selected, notice that they all will abide by the rule that each side will have the same amount of time to present constructive arguments, question the other team (if in the format), and respond in rebuttals.

The "Clash" Process in Debate

Every Moment Counts

Within this time framework, the affirmative tries to compel the audience to agree that the resolution should be adopted. The support for the resolution means that either the audience should accept the affirmative team's judgments on a value-oriented topic, or it should agree that the future action suggested by the policy topic should be taken. The negative attempts to prevent the affirmative from succeeding. Since time is limited in a debate, it is literally true that every moment counts. Time is precious to the speaker. No time can be wasted. If you waste a minute aimlessly repeating yourself, it is a minute which can never be made up in that debate. If your opponent has spent one minute introducing three items of evidence against your case, you have lost out twice.

Moreover, a debate can be extremely confusing to an audience. Any human being who listens for forty-eight or sixty minutes to four other people arguing is probably going to be swamped by conflicting ideas. To the listener, there is too much time in a debate—that is, so many things are said during the debate that the listener finds it extremely difficult to keep track of what is going on.

Think and Speak in Outline Terms

For these two reasons—the speaker's need for time and the audience's saturation with it—it is imperative that every debate speaker know exactly what to try to do at every instant of the debate. This awareness of what is going on must be communicated to the listeners as well. Therefore, the first principle of successful debate speaking is: think and speak in outline terms.

In other words, debate speakers must know what the main ideas are in the debate so they can tell the audience what they are. Obviously, if the debaters do not know their own main arguments, they will never be able to recognize those of the opposition.

The easiest way to visualize this principle in practice is to see the entire debate as two outlines set alongside each other. To think in outline terms is to view the debate case in terms of its functional parts: issues, arguments, and evidence. For instance, in a debate on a particular policy proposition, the affirmative might outline part of their case as follows:

ISSUE:	I. The present system of state and federal highways is inadequate, for:
ARGUMENT:	A. United States highways are substandard for present needs, for:
EVIDENCE:	1. Specific supporting evidence
	2. Specific supporting evidence
	3. Specific supporting evidence
ARGUMENT:	B. Expansion under the present system is not adequate for future needs, because:
EVIDENCE:	1. Specific supporting evidence
	2. Specific supporting evidence
	3. Specific supporting evidence
	4. Specific supporting evidence
ARGUMENT:	C. Present federal help is inadequate, for:
EVIDENCE:	1. Specific supporting evidence
	2. Specific supporting evidence
ARGUMENT:	D. Present highway programs do not provide work projects to alleviate unemployment, because:
EVIDENCE:	1. Specific supporting evidence
	2. Specific supporting evidence
	3. Specific supporting evidence

If the audience heard only this speech, well-delivered and with the use of adequate evidence (sufficient and compelling), they would be expected to agree with the speaker. Such a speech, by the affirmative, would contain what is called a *prima facie case*. Likewise, a speaker presenting a well-organized and supported first affirmative on a value-oriented topic, which presents sufficient and compelling reasons to believe the value judgment is clear and applicable, would also have presented a prima facie case for the adoption of the resolution.

The Prima Facie Case and the Debate Clash

Debaters use the term *case* to mean all the assembled proof available for demonstrating the truth of the proposition (for the affirmative) or the untruth of the proposition (for the negative). A complete outline of a case is called a *brief*.

The Prima Facie Case

The affirmative presents a collection of assertions and proofs sufficient to create belief in the proposition. This obligation is true for fact, value, and policy propositions. Suppose that no negative speaker were to appear; would it still be possible that when the first affirmative finished speaking, the audience would remain unconvinced? Speakers can lose by default if they fail to create belief in what they say. The term *prima facie* means, literally, at first appearance or on the face of things. Technically, in a debate, it means a case which establishes such a high degree of probability that the proposition must be accepted unless refuted. Thus, the clash is set up for us—the affirmative must offer a reasonably compelling case, and the negative is obligated to respond with refutation.

Establishing the Clash Areas

In a debate, of course, there is an opposing team of speakers. How should the first negative speaker reply? For the sake of clarity, the negative must also visualize their speeches in outline form. When the first negative finishes speaking, then, the audience might have the following opposing sets of outlines to consider:

Affirmative	*Negative*
I. The present system of state and	I. The affirmative has said

federal highways is inadequate for four reasons:

A. U.S. highways are substandard for present needs, for:
   1. Evidence
   2. Evidence
   3. Evidence
B. Expansion under the present system is not adequate for future needs, for:
   1. Evidence
   2. Evidence
   3. Evidence
   4. Evidence

C. Present federal help is not adequate:
   1. Evidence
   2. Evidence

D. Present highway programs do not provide work projects to alleviate unemployment:
   1. Evidence
   2. Evidence
   3. Evidence

there are four deficiencies in the present system. We shall now review each reason from the negative perspective.

A. American highways are the best in the world:
   1. Evidence
   2. Evidence

B. Expansion is suited to future needs:

   1. Evidence
   2. Evidence
   3. Evidence
   4. Evidence
   5. Evidence
C. Federal help is adequate:
   1. Evidence
   2. Evidence
   3. Evidence
D. Unemployment is not a real issue:

   1. Evidence

If this pattern has been followed, two things have happened in the debate:

1. The speakers have shown the audience the opposing arguments and, therefore, they have asked the audience to make a decision on the basis of evidence. The clash between ideas has been set up. It is now up to each side to show why its own conclusions should be accepted, on the basis of the proofs it can show the audience.

2. The negative speaker has declared that the negative team will not discuss the question of unemployment as a major idea. This serves to narrow the debate to its essential points and heightens the clash between the two teams. The speaker has defined by exclusion the area of clash between the two teams.

How to Budget Time in the Clash Process

If the speakers realize that they must constantly be aware of their own arguments and those of the opponents, they will soon decide that they must not overlook any major ideas which might persuade their audience. They face two difficult tasks. First, they must have a clear idea of what they want the audience to accept. Second, they must speak in such a way that the audience never becomes confused. The first affirmative speaker has little to worry about in this respect because no other speaker has yet appeared to confuse the issues. The first affirmative also has the advantage of careful preparation and rehearsal of the speech so that each idea can be expressed exactly as planned. But each of the following speakers has a problem. By the time the last rebuttal presenter stands up to speak, for example, seven previous speeches have been delivered, using perhaps from eight thousand to nine thousand words in all. Add to that the four cross-examination periods with their questions and answers, and the possibilities for confusion are obvious.

Therefore, all debate speakers must speak in terms of a double outline—the outline of their own case and the outline of their opponents. They budget their time, consequently, so that they are able at every major point to tell the audience what is going on. And they cannot thus enlighten the audience unless they have decided in their own minds exactly how much attention each idea is worth. Some sort of overall time plan is necessary.

Since each of the four speakers in a team debate faces a slightly different problem, each one has a different time budget. The following chart shows a normal time-budgeting plan based on the time limits used in typical high school and college debates.

Speakers' Duties

The approximate minimum duties of the various speakers in their constructive and rebuttal speeches are outlined below. While these are simply suggestions for speech plans, they provide a fairly useful and typical guide for debate speakers, whether just beginners or advanced champions. Once a plan is chosen by the team, it should be followed as closely as possible. Avoid wasting time during the debate by attempting to create new plans or major modifications under the pressure of the time clock. The times suggested indicate both a job which needs to be done during the speech and a maximum allotment to that job.

Constructive Speeches

First Affirmative	Time	First Negative	Time
1. Define terms/criteria	1 min.	1. Refutation (last chance on definition)	2 min.
2. Outline (preview) entire case, including partner's	30 sec.	2. Outline (preview) entire negative case	30 sec.
3. Develop main case	6 min.	3. Develop main case	5 min.
4. Summarize	30 sec.	4. Summarize	30 sec.
	8 min.		8 min.

Second Affirmative		Second Negative	
1. Respond to challenge on terms/criteria	2 min.	1. Outline affirmative refuting main points	2 min.
2. Repeat outline of affirmative case and refute negative case points, showing points negative ignored or failed to refute	2 min.	2. Repeat negative case outline, showing conflict with affirmative case and indicating points unrefuted by affirmative	2 min.
3. Extend and re-establish affirmative case	3½ min.	3. Extend and re-establish negative case	3½ min.
4. Summarize	30 sec.	4. Summarize	30 sec.
	8 min.		8 min.

Rebuttals

Each rebuttal speech follows the same plan whether the speaker is affirmative or negative. The two speakers on a side must split the outline between them, as in preparing a constructive case.

First Rebuttal

1. Point out (outline) main points of opponents' entire case and list which one your partner will take   30 sec.

2. Refute approximately one-half of points   3 min.

3. Summarize your team case   30 sec.

Second Rebuttal

1. Follow plan outline for second negative speaker in constructive speeches, covering approximately one-half of points remaining in 3½ minutes, saving at least 30 seconds for a summary of entire case and compare with opponents.

Understanding the Debate Process

If the speakers understand what they are trying to do at every stage of the debate and clarify the natural clash of ideas for the audience, the audience can then devote its attention to making an intelligent judgment based on the reasoning and evidence which each side brings forth. The whole purpose of public debate, as noted earlier, is to provide an opportunity for a rational consideration of alternatives. If the speakers confuse themselves and the audience, the entire debate is a waste of time. To avoid such confusion, it is essential that the debaters understand what they are trying to do. It is also essential that they budget their time, think in outline terms, and identify the main issues while casting aside the minor ones. Above all, they must remind the audience of what is going on. We call this obligation the *burden of communication*, which all speakers carry.

If speakers understand the debate process itself, they are then able to think more intelligently about the problem of *proof*. That is, they must consider how to persuade an audience to accept a statement which they make. Even if the audience is a single judge in a classroom during a tournament, acceptance of argument is still the goal. The debate structure is the skeleton of the arguments, and the proofs are its muscle.

This section has introduced you to some of the basic concepts and vocabulary associated with scholastic debate. Some of the initial concerns have been brought out, and some of the formats, propositions, duties, and times have been discussed. Review this introduction now, so that you will be ready to move to the next step of building the debate case.

3

Building the Debate Case

Underlying Concepts

More than two thousand years ago, Aristotle identified the debater's basic problem as follows:

> There are only two parts to a speech: You make a statement and you prove it.

In modern debating, the two teams make a statement, in effect, when they agree to uphold either the affirmative or the negative side. The whole debating structure—the sequence of speeches, four on each side—is designed to make sure that each speaker has an equal chance to make a statement and to prove it.

When the debate process itself has been understood, then the basic questions to be answered are: "What is proof?" and "How is proof used in a debate?"

The Problem of Proof

Creating Belief

It is an obvious fact that merely stating a proposition will not cause listeners to accept it. If you say, "We should spend more money for highway construction," all you have done is to assert that such a step should be taken. From the audience's point of view, you have only raised the question, "Why should we?" No person in that audience has any reason to believe that the proposal is good simply because you have voiced it. If, however, you are able to say, "Because. . . ." and then list several reasons why each of your listeners should honestly make the same statement, you are likely to succeed in proving your point. You have succeeded when it is possible for your audience to make the same assertion that you do; when every audience member, if asked, would say, "Yes, we should spend more money for highway construction."

This apparently simple relationship—that is, the agreement between speaker and audience—is the key to the whole problem of debate. If you can create belief in your statements, you can secure this agreement. *Proof*, therefore, may be defined as whatever tends to create belief. This proof may encompass anything from the speaker's appearance, apparent sincerity, tone of voice, or the speech itself. However, since every speaker tries to appear sincere and interested in the subject, the debate situation focuses attention on the speech itself. Hence, for all practical purposes, the term *proof* means those items of evidence and reasoning which tend to make an audience agree with the assertions. *Evidence* can be defined as matters of fact or opinion which tend to support those assertions. On the other hand, *reasoning* is the process of inferring relationships between the evidence and the assertions. The mere listing of facts or the reading of evidence cards or the piling up of opinions, therefore, is not enough to create belief—the audience must be shown an explicit, logical relationship between these things and the assertion at hand.

The Toulmin Model

Stephen Toulmin, a philosopher, rhetorician, and logician has described the process of proof in terms of three areas which lead an audience through the reasoning process. He calls these areas: data, warrant, and claim.

Data are the items of information you gather and process. You can think of these items as evidence in a debate. They can be the examples, quotations, statistics, or other materials which you use to build your analysis. On the basis of these data, you ask the audience to accept your *claim*.

The claim is the end of the reasoning process, and it is your conclusion, or in debate, your assertion. Several arguments become the data for an issue, and the issues become the reasons to support the proposition. Thus, the debate is structured so that there are interrelated series of claims, each backed by data. The way we connect these materials together, our linking of ideas, is called the *warrant*.

The warrant is the reasoning process by which we look at one bit of information (data) and decide what it means (claim). Sometimes logic provides the warrants for our conclusions, other times the warrants are hard to find, illogical, or even missing altogether. In a debate, the reasoning process becomes the warrant and is often overlooked when searching for problems with your own case or that of your opponents. It is easier to see data, and thus many debaters simply try to attack the evidence. It is also easy to see the claims, since they are major headings of the case outline. Warrants, or reasons to connect information, are much more difficult to locate, and we encourage you to keep looking for the underlying reasons or assumptions which you and other debaters use.

An easy way to think of the reasoning process in the Toulmin model is in the following diagram:

In addition to this simple introduction, Toulmin also describes limitations to the data which might call for supports. There are also limitations to the claim. These are qualifiers and reservations about the extent of the claim or the circumstances under which the claim might not be correct. The warrant may also need to have support. A good follow-up to this brief introduction to the very useful Toulmin system could be found in many contemporary argumentation and logic books.

Burdens in Debate

Three more terms should be understood by the debater at this point:

Burden of proof is a primary rule of any argument or debate. It first requires the affirmative to bear the burden of proving the proposition. Subsequently, it requires every speaker to support each assertion. Because any assertion must be supported by proofs, "those who assert must prove" is a fundamental and long-standing rule of every debate.

Burden of rebuttal is the second rule of debate which is shared by all speakers. It requires that a speaker reply to an assertion which is supported by sufficient proofs. If opposing speakers do not reply, the audience may legitimately agree with the original presenter of the assertion and therefore reject the second speaker's case. The failure to respond may be taken as granting the assertion (and thus the argument or issue) to the original presenter.

Burden of communication is the third key term to be understood by every debater. We have already mentioned this concept several times in previous sections, however, it bears repeating. Each speaker is obligated to communicate issues, arguments, and evidence to the audience. If the debaters are only talking among themselves, it does little good. If they use shorthand abbreviations, jargon, and incomplete references and citations, they are failing to communicate clearly to the audience. As in the other two burdens, each speaker carries and must uphold the burden of communication by: following the outline format suggested; identifying the issues and arguments along the way through the use of clear transitions, previews, and reviews; and speaking at a tone and rate which enables the audience to follow and to respond.

These three burdens are carried initially by the first affirmative and then by *every* speaker who follows. These three burdens are part of every debate proposition of fact, of value, or of policy. The speaker who fails to carry every one of these burdens also fails to carry the debate.

As noted earlier, when a speaker advances a proposition for acceptance (for instance, that we should increase our highway building), the audience can merely raise the question, "Why should we?" The burden of proof for the affirmative at this point becomes the necessity of answering that question. But after the affirmative speaker has presented reasons for the audience to agree with the statement, the audience in a sense turns to the negative and says, "Well, why not?" The burden of rebuttal initially falls to the negative requiring them to answer that second question in order to prevent the audience from accepting the affirmative's position. Both teams must carry the burden of communication from the first speech forward. This burden becomes more difficult as the debate progresses, for the number of issues and arguments increases and the time limits shrink. Nevertheless, the burden of communication must be met for either team to have impact on the decision.

A final note of caution is in order before we turn to the uses of proof in actual debate. We defined proof as whatever tends to create belief. A speaker dealing with a proposition of value is dealing with areas of subjectivity and relative merits. The speaker in a policy-oriented debate is dealing with future action, prediction, and forecast. Therefore, neither speaker can offer absolute proofs. They are dealing in the realm of probability, of reasonableness, and of comparative worth, not in certainty. Some debaters are distressed to find that their opponents offer arguments which seem just as good as their own, but this result is perfectly natural in a discussion which is essentially seeking a choice or judgment between two or more possible alternatives or evaluations.

Obviously, then, no single argument in a debate is likely to be conclusive by itself. No single proof is likely to settle the whole discussion. Therefore, the debater must be prepared to use a wide variety of arguments and evidence in order to make sure (or more probable) that the audience will accept the overall case.

As the debate speakers prepare for the debate, then, they face an extremely complex series of problems: understanding the debate proposition, outlining their own and their colleague's approach to the case, collecting proofs, and even anticipating attacks by the opponents. The problems are complex, but each speaker's preparation can be simplified if this entire process of assertion and proof is understood in terms of four elements involved in debate.

Four Elements in Debate

Structural Elements as Basic Concepts

There are four structural elements that serve as the ingredients of a debate case. These are: (1) proposition, (2) issues, (3) arguments, and (4) evidence. Analysis of a debate case is made possible through a complete understanding of the function of these parts. A fifth element, and the most important one, is the reasoning process. It, however, is not a separate element so much as the means by which the other four are bound together. The following paragraphs will serve to define each of these four formal elements, while the subsequent section will apply each element directly to the complex problem of building a debate case.

Proposition. A *proposition* (or *resolution*) is a judgment expressed in a declarative sentence. Each debate centers around a carefully-worded proposition in order that everyone may know precisely what is being talked about. As we noted in chapter 2, there are propositions about fact, value, and policy. The value or policy propositions are usually used in school debate, and both are supported by three formal elements: issues, arguments, and evidence.

Issues. *Issues* are often called inherently vital points. They are the *assertions* (or *unsupported statements*) which must be proved in order to establish that the proposition ought to be adopted. They are the main contentions that function as the basic reasons for the adoption of the proposition. Finding the issues that are relevant to a proposition is the result of analysis. Ordinary intelligence will suggest that if one advocates a change from the present system (status quo), it becomes necessary to support the idea that there is something wrong with the status quo or that some major new benefit will result from the change.

In a policy proposition, if these faults or benefits are extensive, they may provide sufficient and compelling reason for concluding that there is a need to change from the present system. In short, the fact that there is a need to change becomes an issue. If you are dealing with a value proposition, then common sense also tells you that you must also provide your listeners with enough reasons to conclude that the evaluation you are making should be accepted by them as well. Issues do not stand by themselves; rather, they appear as assertions and need to be supported with arguments and evidence.

Arguments.   An *argument* is an assertion which is the result of reasoning. The characteristic feature of argument, as compared to other discourse, is that it states or implies a reasoning process. For example: "The papers are on the table" is not an argument; but the statement, "If we do not close the window, the papers will be blown off the table" is an argument because it contains an inference, the result of a reasoning process. Arguments serve as reasons for the acceptance of an issue. Arguments may stand by themselves but usually need to be supported with evidence.

Evidence.   *Evidence* is that statement of fact or opinion which makes an assertion acceptable to an audience. In debate, evidence serves as a means to an end. The end may be called belief, conviction, or proof. Evidence has often been called the raw material of proof. Indeed, all relevant matters of fact and opinion should serve as the basis of every debater's reasoning. These carefully selected and cited facts and opinions are the debater's evidence.

Example: Function of the Four Elements
In the previous chapter you saw an example of an outline of an affirmative case on highways along with a companion negative outline on the same topic. Here is another example of a hypothetical case outline which uses these four elements in a value-oriented topic.

PROPOSITION: Resolved: That the United States would be justified in significantly increasing trade restrictions.

ISSUE: I. National security considerations would justify increasing trade restrictions, for:

ARGUMENT: A. Highly technical products reach our adversaries.

EVIDENCE: 1. Secretary of State testimony regarding loss of important computer advances to communist world

    2. Defense Department report on military equipment sold through third parties

ARGUMENT: B. Technical losses endanger our security.

EVIDENCE: 1. Congressional hearing citation regarding uses made of our technology by others which have harmed U.S. security

    2. Statement from Joint Chiefs of Staff concerning danger to our military personnel resulting from technical transfers

ISSUE: II. Domestic Industries Need Protection, for:

ARGUMENT: A. The textile industry has been hurt by imports.

EVIDENCE: 1. Statistics on lost jobs in textiles due to imports

    2. Etc.

Etc. . . .

Thus you can see how the relationship of each of these elements is present in a value-oriented topic as well as in policy questions. The rule is simple—all propositions are supported by major issues, and these in turn are supported by arguments which have specific evidence as their supports. All of these elements are bound together by reasoning—a fifth and ever-present element.

When you read chapter 5, do not forget this relationship because you will need to create both affirmative and negative cases from outlines, and the format above gives you the outline system

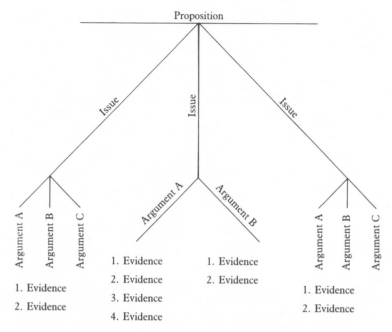

Fig. 3.1. Relationship of the four elements

to follow. You might also remember figure 3.1, which represents a schematic relationship among the four structural elements of any debate.

As you can see, the debate case is built upon evidence. Good supporting materials, in the form of fact, opinion, and reasoning, which the audience will find compelling, are the foundation of every debate case.

Where do speakers find good evidence? Which materials do they select for use? How do they record information so they can use it later? These questions will be answered in chapter 4 so that you can gain an introduction to the process of research. Use this method to seek and record information about your debate topics and any other topics you need to research. Many students find it beneficial to do term papers, reports, and even master's theses and doctoral dissertations using the research skills learned in debate.

Summary of the Relationship of the Four Elements

1. The proposition is supported by main contentions, called issues.
2. The issues, which appear as assertions, are supported by reasoned discourse, called arguments.
3. The arguments are supported with the best available evidence.

4

Research and Reasoning

Acquiring Knowledge and Developing Proof

Acquiring Knowledge

The Value of Research

Research is both a first step and a continuing process for the debate speaker. It is the first step in preparation because sound analysis of issues and arguments is possible only when the speaker has acquired a thorough background of knowledge relevant to the proposition. Initially, a debater needs to think about the topic: what areas are suggested, what terms are presented which need to be defined or analyzed. The implications of the topic area are important to think about and to discuss with others who are also concerned with the topic. Once this general grounding in the topic is developed, you can begin to focus your efforts. The following materials are offered as a guide to research.

Bibliographical Aids

The first step in research is to find out what references are available on the subject being investigated. The use of a bibliography is the most efficient method of discovering relevant materials. There are at least three advantages to the use of a bibliography:

(1) a bibliography tends to be a selected list of references that usually includes only the best material available; (2) it often provides an estimate of the value of a book or article, either by an annotation or by a reference to a critical review; and (3) it allows the debater to see the available references as a whole and gives direction to the debater's subsequent research.

The debate speaker may ask how to go about finding bibliographies on a specific question. The answer is that the needs of the researcher have been anticipated and guides to bibliographies have been compiled. These works are arranged according to subject headings and will indicate what bibliographies are available for the particular subject under investigation. A list of bibliographies and other reference materials chosen for their particular relevance to debate research are included in this book.

Reading

The debater's reading should be guided by the principle that reading should progress from the general to the specific. This principle is based on the well-founded assumption that the investigator must have some grasp of the general problem before being able to intelligently evaluate its specific aspects. The method is consistent with other aspects of the debater's preparation: attention focuses first on issues, then on supporting arguments, and then on specific forms of evidence.

Reading, therefore, begins with the best available general works (probably a standard book together with an accepted research report); proceeds to references on specific aspects of the problem (probably articles in periodicals); and finally, surveys other books, articles, research reports, and newspaper accounts to accumulate specific evidence. A second guiding principle related to reading is that issues must first be discovered; next, arguments must be developed; and finally, attention must be centered on the gathering of evidence. An efficient practice is to survey each source briefly before beginning the actual reading and before taking any reading notes.

Note Taking

Because debaters cannot carry all their references with them (though some appear to be trying), they need to take notes on the material they read. The debaters are thus immediately faced with the problem of knowing when to record data. In the process of research, debaters will find that materials come in no logical order; an apparently valuable group of statistics may be encountered in the first general reference work that is read. At this point the debaters may not know how the evidence will be used, nor will they be certain it is valuable. While discretion must be used, it is a good idea to record all materials that seem to be valuable. It is better to record too much than too little. The problem will diminish as the debater acquires a knowledgeable background in the subject.

Guiding Principles of Note Taking:

1. Write your notes as though you were writing them for someone else.
2. Record enough information so that its meaning will be clear weeks and months later. Assume that your source will not be available to you again.
3. Record only *one* item on each card.
4. Use a consistent form that includes full bibliographical information. The Modern Language Association style is suggested as the standard academic system for footnotes, bibliographical citations, and paper formats.
5. Be consistent in the type of card you use for your notes. A four-by-six-inch index card is probably the minimum size to be useful and is the one most debaters actually use in tournaments.
6. Reread your notes:
   a. so that you will assimilate the results of your research. Such an assimilation of ideas will facilitate both the composition and delivery of your arguments during the debate process.
   b. so that items not useful can be discarded.

The importance of good note taking cannot be emphasized too much. Your future success and progress as a debater depend absolutely on the quality of information you begin with. You base your analysis of issues, your development of arguments, and your assertions of support on the information you read and record. Accurate recording of notes will allow you to develop quality materials in subsequent work sessions. On the other hand, inaccurate or sloppy note taking can lead you to build erroneous assumptions later on, and if you present faulty information in a debate tournament and claim it is true and accurate, you may be forced to forfeit the round in which you used the erroneous evidence. You could even be completely removed from the competition or banned from participating in subsequent rounds or future tournaments. The penalty for using inaccurate evidence is so severe that you should be aware of it now and guard against any accidental misuse of evidence by ensuring that you take clear and accurate notes, with complete citation (see figure 4.1).

With an index card such as in figure 4.1, you can easily see what category of information you are dealing with and can also instantly provide a complete citation for use in a discussion, a

REASONS WHY UNITED NATIONS EFFECTIVENESS WILL NOT IMPROVE

Ernest B. Haas—Professor of Political Science, UC-Berkeley
International Organization
Spring 1983
p. 189

Instead of routinized mediation and peacekeeping activities, large public conferences have become the preferred way of managing conflict. The major powers no longer exercise leadership in conflict management, the role of the secretariats has declined, and financial and political disagreements militate against the mounting of operations to keep the peace and supervise truce agreements.

Fig. 4.1. Sample note card.

tournament, or in response to a challenge if need be. It is important to realize that *you* are responsible for all evidence you use, even if you did not personally locate or copy it from the original. If you have copied materials from another, then you become responsible for it later on, so make certain that you copy accurately and that you double check the original as soon as you can. If, in a tournament, you happen to use a card which is inaccurate, it will do you no good to say, "Well, it is not my fault, I copied this from a teammate." You, not the teammate, will incur the penalty. Accuracy thus helps your friends when they review your materials, and if everyone on the team is following the same standards for accuracy and completeness, your entire team will benefit.

Interviews

After the debater has acquired a basic background of knowledge on the question, it is often helpful to discuss the problems under consideration with a person who has had special training and experience in the subject. Local colleges and universities may have such experts on their faculty, or there may be government offices or research institutions or special interest groups who have personnel knowledgeable in the area. You may wish to make an appointment to interview the expert, and several members of your team might like to go. As in any good interview, a specific appointment, a series of well-thought-out questions, and plenty of note paper, pencils, or even a tape recorder will help you obtain a successful interview.

Discussion

The value of discussion as preparation for debate can hardly be overestimated. In discussing ideas with others, the debater becomes aware of new facets to the problem and new ideas concerning the solution. And, as a practical advantage, the debaters have an opportunity to exchange information among themselves. While a general discussion may be valuable in the preliminary stages of preparation, the most valuable discussions usually center about a particular aspect of the proposition for debate. A good 'coaching session' may consist of a series of such discussions, each with a preplanned and announced topic area. That way, each debater can come to the session with relevant materials, ideas, questions, and contributions.

Organizing Materials for Reference

The debater who has conducted careful investigation of the subject should then organize and file the results of the research systematically. Careful organization at this point will facilitate the development of the case and will subsequently be of invaluable aid in the process of debate.

When to Organize. The organization of materials for reference should be delayed until the debater has a thorough enough background in the subject to see it as a whole. Until this point in preparation is reached, the debater is unable to apply useful subject headings to the note cards. Preliminary headings should, therefore, be penciled on the cards and revised as the research develops.

How to Organize. There are two common methods of organizing materials for reference. One method uses a loose-leaf notebook and arranges all the materials the debater will use— outlines of constructive speeches, an indexed section of evidence and rebuttal cards, and rebuttal note sheets—in one place. The use of the notebook method requires extremely careful organization but has the obvious advantage of keeping all the debater's materials in one place. An obvious disadvantage is that reading notes are most conveniently taken on index cards, and these are difficult to incorporate into the notebook system. Even the best of the currently available plastic sheets are often cumbersome or inadequate or expensive. The most common method is to use a file box containing index cards and subject heading dividers. Some debaters use a combination of these, keeping their case outlines, rebuttal sheets, and most frequently used evidence cards in a notebook, and the larger amount of remaining information in an accompanying file box. The more you advance in debating, the more you will develop a system which works for you.

What to Organize. Most debaters will wish to have two kinds of notes for reference. The first kind is the evidence note, an objective statement of fact or opinion that may be used as the requirements of the occasion demand. Most reference cards will be of this type. A second kind of note is the rebuttal card. These cards are prepared in anticipation of arguments that will need to be refuted. By using rebuttal cards, the debater can prepare in advance what appears to be the best supporting evidence for an answer. In the process of the debate, the speaker who has prepared in this manner need not hurriedly think up an answer to an objection. Instead, the speaker merely reviews the thoughtful answer which has been prepared in advance.

A Comment on Debate Handbooks

As an alternative to research, some debaters depend on the use of cheap, mimeographed, or photocopied handbooks which include affirmative and negative briefs as well as an assortment of evidence. While most teams purchase a few of these items, very few use them to replace research. Debaters who confine their research to these predigested materials will lose much of the value of the debate experience and training. Training you to be able to do competent research on your own is a valuable skill which cannot be purchased or bought. In addition, handbook users lose the creative pleasure of discovering for themselves, and the dull debating done by these people reflects their lack of initiative. Glance through a team copy for ideas, formats, and even to build a bibliography for your own further investigation. Handbooks can give you a start, but debate offers students an opportunity to master techniques of research that will be invaluable whenever they are called upon to investigate, to analyze, to select, and to report. You will be asked to do these things throughout all academic undertakings and in most careers which require intellectual activity. Handbook users lose this valuable training. If handbooks are used wisely, they are hardly used at all.

You have seen some of the techniques for acquiring supporting materials, but how do you decide what to select and what to overlook? One of the best ways to know what to do is to understand the nature of proof as it builds support for issues and arguments. The next section discusses proof and how you can build it out of your research and reasoning.

Developing Proof

Supporting Issues

In a debate case, each of the issues appears as an assertion. Together they form a group of contentions which, if proved, ought to lead to the adoption of the affirmative proposal. Two formal elements provide the basis of support for the issues: reasoned arguments are the elements that directly support the issues; evidence is the raw material upon which the reasoning is based. If you have followed the suggestions in the section above, you have begun to gather information, knowledge, and evidence about the topic. That information provides you with ideas, and in some cases you have drawn or are beginning to draw some inferences or conclusions from this evidence. The following material considers the use of arguments and evidence as you prepare to construct your affirmative and negative cases. Whether you are debating a proposition of fact, value, or policy, the fundamental processes for reasoning from evidence are the same.

Arguments

Arguments appear in the debate case as reasons for the support of an issue. In the example outlined below, three arguments are used in supporting an issue of need.

Example: Use of Arguments to Support Need Issues
    I. There is a need to change from the present policy of nuclear testing and development, for:
        A. The present policy is, in effect, an arms race and experience indicates that the build-up of arms leads to war, for:

      1. 1910–1914 example

      2. 1933–1939 example

B. If the present policy continues, the world population will be subjected to the dangers of radiation, for:

      1. Statistical evidence

      2. Authoritative evidence

C. Either testing and development is discontinued now, or the dangers will increase, and future control will be more difficult to achieve, for:

      1. Many other nations will be in possession of nuclear weapons.

         a. Statistical evidence

         b. Authoritative evidence

      2. Inspection and control would therefore be more difficult and costly.

      3. The danger of the irrational use of nuclear weapons would increase.

The Fundamentals of Argumentation

The debate speaker may profitably spend a semester or more in the formal study of argumentation—the process of reasoning and analysis. The following principles are offered only as basic fundamentals and introduction to the terms which may serve as a useful guide in the analysis of argument.

Reasoned Discourse. The reasoning process puts previously unrelated facts and opinions (evidence) into a new relationship and draws a conclusion from that relationship. Each of the arguments cited is the result of such a process of reasoning. As the debate speaker presents assertions, together with supporting evidence, argumentative speaking or reasoned discourse results.

Generalizations. Although debaters will give a particular application to their arguments, their reasoning will either assert a general principle or will be derived from a general principle. These principles are called generalizations. Such common assertions as "If Amy baked the bread, it will be good," implies the generalization that "All bread baked by Amy is good." The generalizations may or may not be sound. Perhaps the most useful guiding principle for debaters to remember as they analyze argument is that *every argument either makes a generalization or proceeds from one.* Inductive argument examines the real world of physical things or of human experience and makes a generalization about it. Scientific investigation, for example, proceeds from the observation of particular instances (examples) to the assertion of general principles. Deductive argument, on the other hand, proceeds from these generalizations and may or may not state the generalization upon which the argument is based. The guiding principle for the testing of any argument is to find and evaluate the generalization upon which the argument is based.

In policy debates, the descriptions of goals or the conclusions about how the current policy system works, or should work, are common generalizations about which the debate revolves. In value-oriented debate, statements of goals or value principles which people hold, or ought to hold, provide the generalizations for specific arguments for those debates.

Forms of Argument.   The inductive or deductive argument may appear in a variety of forms. Nevertheless, because of the requirements for clarity in the organization of a debate case, the debate speaker usually states the assertions first and then proves them. In short, debaters usually use a deductive model for the exposition of their arguments. The previous example concerning nuclear testing used three forms of deductive argument in supporting the need issue in a policy-oriented example. They were:

1. "The present policy constitutes an arms race, and experience indicates that the build-up of armaments leads to war." This generalization is termed a categorical argument because it asserts that all of one thing (armament build-ups) leads to another thing (war). A way to state this categorical argument would be through the generalization, "All arms races lead to war." If this generalization is dependable, then the argument is sound.

2. "If the present policy continues, then the world population will be subjected to the dangers of radiation." This hypothetical or conditional argument is different from the one above because it asserts its conclusion in a more tentative way than did the categorical one. It uses the "if . . . then" construction, which marks the argument as conditional. If the first part happens, then the second part will follow. If the first part does not come about, then the second will not follow. This hypothetical or conditional argument could be stated, "If the policy continues, then there will be dangers of radiation."

3. "Either testing or development is discontinued now, or the dangers will increase. . . ." This third argument is called disjunctive because it asserts that one thing will happen or another thing will happen. Disjunctive arguments are marked by the use of the "either . . . or" construction in their generalizations. The underlying generalization for this disjunctive argument would be phrased, "Either testing is discontinued, or greater dangers will follow."

The three types of argument, categorical, hypothetical, and disjunctive, comprise the basic units of our reasoning process. In each case, whether you are arguing about values or about policies, you must draw the impact of the argument for your listeners. In order to demonstrate how your argument has value in their decision, you need to indicate the generalization from which your argument was developed. The value of any argument, therefore, depends upon the quality of the generalization it is based upon. To grasp the generalization is to see the essence of the argument, any argument. Debate speakers are often prone merely to quibble about some third-level evidence supporting an argument when they should instead deal with the second-level—the argument itself, or the primary basis for the argument—the underlying generalization. If you deal with the connections, or lack of connections, between generalizations, arguments, and evidence, you are demonstrating that you can debate about the reasoning process and about the errors your opponents may have made in that process. Such arguments are always more impressive and have far greater impact on the judges' decisions than do minor attacks about the date or qualifications of a source or any counter sources.

This discussion is not to say that evidence is unimportant to the quality of your debating, but to emphasize the fundamental place which reasoning plays in your thinking and communication of ideas. Once you have the reasoning process under control and can identify the links, or lack thereof, in an argument, then you are ready to fill in the supporting evidence as the third part of this chain.

The Relationship of Evidence to Argument. Arguments are based upon evidence. To reason in debate is to consider the meaning of facts and opinions. Generalizations emerge from the consideration of evidence—how you connect scattered ideas, facts, and opinions into a coherent series of justifiable conclusions. *Fallacies*, or errors in reasoning, result from drawing unjustified implications from the evidence. Argument concerns the meaning of evidence, the manner in which facts are related in order to produce a conclusion. The four kinds of arguments stated below illustrate four relationships of factual material.

1. The argument from *sign* asserts that if fact A exists, it is a reliable indication that fact B also exists. A sign is like a clue. The fact that Jo's car is parked outside her house may be taken as a sign that Jo is home. The sign argument is based on the generalization that all cases of A are indications of B. Sign arguments affirm that an assertion is true. The debate speaker typically uses argument from sign to establish that a problem exists or that a value is held.

2. The *causal* argument asserts that if fact A exists, it will cause fact B to follow. The fact that Jo's car ran out of gas may be taken as a cause for her car to stop. The causal argument is based on the generalization that all cases of A will be followed by B. These arguments are very strong if you can establish the connective link between A and B. Asserting such a causal link is easy, but proving it is difficult because so many *B's* do not simply

have a single cause *A* to point to, instead they probably have a variety of causes.

Causal arguments declare why an assertion is true. The debate speaker uses causal arguments to establish why the problem exists and why the proposed solution will work or why a certain value structure exists and what the impacts of having such a value would be.

3. The argument from *analogy* asserts that if the facts relating to A and the facts relating to B are alike in certain known respects, they will also be alike in another respect. From the fact that Jo's 1985 Toyota gets 35 MPG, the conclusion may be drawn that my 1985 Toyota will also get 35 MPG.

Arguments from analogy are based on the generalization that if specific instances are compared and found to be alike in a number of essential and relevant respects, they will also be alike in others, particularly the one under discussion. The problem is that all analogies are ultimately false, for no two things or circumstances are ever exactly alike. If they were exactly alike, they would be the same thing. The debater must establish that the similarities are close enough to be significant. For this reason, analogy is best used to clarify or add interest since it is weak in establishing proof.

4. The argument from *example* is the reasoning process that provides the generalizations upon which the deductive arguments are based. After observing Jo wash her car each Saturday morning for six weeks, you might generalize that Jo always washes her car on Saturday mornings.

The argument from example asserts a generalization. The debate speaker uses examples to support general assertions on which causal and sign arguments may be based.

As you can begin to appreciate, these different types of arguments are often used in conjunction with each other. The interplay of types is based on the type of argument being offered and the type of support necessary or available. Let us look at supporting materials briefly.

Evidence

One test of argument is the evaluation of the evidence upon which the argument is based. Evidence, as we have seen, consists of facts and opinions and is the raw material upon which the debater's reasoning depends. The function of evidence is to make the debater's assertions apparent. A few guiding principles should be remembered:

1. Use the best evidence available. This means the evidence should be accurate, recent, from a reliable source, readily available and verifiable, generally acceptable to the audience, free from obvious bias, and directly germane to the argument under consideration.

2. Use enough evidence to support your assertions clearly, but have more in reserve.

3. Make your evidence clear by relating it explicitly to the assertion it aims to support.

4. Do not allow your evidence to be questionable. Ideally, the evidence should not be debatable. The facts ought to be as you say they are, the opinions ought to be the assertions of relevant authorities. A debate in which the speakers debate evidence is likely to be a poor contest; conflict should center about the meaning of evidence, its relevance, its impact, or its application. It should not be about its accuracy.

If you follow these guidelines in collecting and using your evidence, you will have a firm foundation for your debating. Make certain that you examine your opponents' use of evidence on the same basis, and if they have been deficient, then you can cast great doubt on the conclusions they infer. Challenges about the accuracy of evidence are a rare and serious event in scholastic debate. Most tournaments and associations will remove debaters from competition who use falsified information. Remember, if you say it, you are responsible for it; and so make certain that any evidence you did not obtain first hand has been verified to your satisfaction—to the degree that you would be willing to stake your debate reputation or career on its authenticity.

Debating about the meaning of evidence is another matter, for it attacks the analysis of the opposition, not their trustworthiness or honesty. Many attacks which challenge evidence are really attacks about the interpretation of evidence and not really about the honesty of the team involved. Be very careful not to confuse the two.

As you can see, evidence is the foundation of good debate for it leads to sound arguments, development of issues and cases, and good refutation. Good research generates good evidence, and so follow the guidelines, even if they seem time consuming at first, because they will pay off as you begin to debate.

Summary

This chapter was designed to introduce you to the basics involved in doing research for debate or any academic undertaking. Some important suggestions were made on how, where, and why to do research. In addition, you also were shown some initial methods for evaluating evidence and some ways to put evidence and ideas together in a form called reasoning. The next step in this process is to put your analysis and reasoning into a format which you can support with the research and evidence you have gathered. That format is called a case, and the next chapter will show you how to organize both affirmative and negative approaches to a debate topic.

5

Constructing Affirmative and Negative Cases

In the previous chapter we talked about the importance of doing quality research so that you would have quality information from which you create your affirmative and negative positions. It is now time to turn your attention to constructing your cases. In a sense, you are always building a new case. As information comes to you and as you consider, analyze, and rethink your ideas and positions, you will constantly modify your cases. For the time being, we will begin with the affirmative case, as it is more focused and more easily grasped.

Constructing the Affirmative Case

Determining the Issues

Debaters who have acquired a knowledgeable background relevant to the proposition are ready to organize the results of their research into a debate case. They should always begin by organizing the affirmative case. Remembering that the issue is the basic element in the support of the proposition, speakers should make their first task to discover what the issues are. To do this, they use the method known as the application of a questionnaire analysis. Since certain issues must be established for any proposition, the questions which suggest these issues are stock, or standard, questions of analysis. They are generally called the *stock issues* of a debate proposition and vary slightly between policy questions and value-oriented questions. Each type of proposition will be discussed separately. Common to each type of proposition is the requirement that all affirmative cases must meet the terms of the topic.

The *topicality issue* is the first test of every case. The question, "Is the affirmative debating the substance of the topic?" must be settled before you decide to go any further. This seemingly simple question can take up the bulk of some debates because analysis can differ. Topicality, as we see it, is not just the clear and reasonable definition of terms, but the application of those definitions in a manner consistent with human experience. While we do not necessarily advocate the "ask the average person on the street what the topic is about" approach to deciding topicality, we do think that asking "the well-informed, educated community of persons who deal in the subject matter" approach is a good way to test the reasonableness of the topic's interpretation chosen by the affirmative. There should always be a variety of approaches to any debate topic. However, if you select an interpretation which pushes the parameters of reason, you may find yourself having to defend the topicality of your case rather than its substance. Thus, debate propositions which deal with policy issues are usually provided by the national committee with a description of parameters to guide debaters and their instructors (and their judges) in evaluating the topicality issue. Value-oriented propositions are usually deliberately phrased in a narrow sense to provide some clarity and guidance. The general rule here is: no matter what kind of topic you work with, you must develop a case which is clearly and defensibly covered by the resolution.

Analyzing Policy Propositions Through Stock Issues

Two general questions are appropriate to the analysis of any proposition of policy. The first asks if there is a problem and the second asks if there is a solution. While these questions, by themselves, are too broad for useful analysis, they form the background for a more precise questionnaire analysis. Typically, five stock issues are used in the analysis of the policy proposition. The first issue aims to analyze the problem and the other four analyze the proposed solution.

The five stock issues are:

   I. Is there a *need* for a change from the status quo?

     A. Does a significant problem exist sufficient to warrant a change?

     B. Does the problem exist as an inherent part of the status quo?

  II. Does the affirmative proposal offer a solution to the problem presented (plan meet need)?

 III. Is the proposal *practical* and *workable?*

 IV. Is the proposal the *best available solution* to the problem?

   V. What are the implications of adopting the proposal?

     A. Does the proposal itself have inherent faults which would create greater problems (disadvantages) than the proposal seeks to alleviate?

     B. Does the proposal have any benefits (advantages)?

In short, the stock issues ask general questions of a proposition in an attempt to discover the material issues, the inherently vital points. When the stock issues are thoughtfully applied by a person who has acquired a knowledgeable background (through the research process suggested in chapter 4) to the question under consideration, relevant arguments will be suggested. The following explanatory material is offered in order to clarify the relationship of the stock issues to the substance of the proposition for debate.

Explaining the Need, or Problem, Issue. The first stock issue asks: Is there a need for a change from the status quo? Analysis proceeds by asking two subsidiary questions:

1. Do sufficient and compelling problems exist to warrant a change from the status quo? It is presumed that no change should be made in present policies unless it can be demonstrated that problems exist in the present situation. Thus, the

need issue seeks to demonstrate that sufficient and compelling reasons (problems) exist to warrant a change. This part of the need contention often revolves on the question of whether there is enough of a problem to constitute a policy change.

2. Why does the problem exist? Does it come from inherent flaws in the status quo? In developing the need issue, many debaters make the error of not going beyond the description of the problem. They reason that because a problem exists, the proposed solution should be adopted. In stopping at this point, they not only treat the need issue superficially, but they fail to discover their most compelling kind of proof—that of causation.

The asking of the simple question, why does a problem exist?, often leads to the essence of the affirmative need issue. When the debaters consider the reasons for the problem, they find themselves viewing the problems themselves as effects and the inherent faults of the status quo as causal factors. At this state of analysis, debaters may develop a compelling need for a change which is based on the inherency of the causal factors of the problems they discuss.

Example: Development of the Need Issue.

Applied to a specific proposition, which we used in earlier examples, the result of the suggested analysis may appear as follows:

Resolved: That the federal government should adopt a new program for the development of the nation's highways.

    I. The present system of state and federal highway development is inadequate, for:

      A. United States highways are substandard for present needs.

        1. ⎧ (Relevant evidence here will include a descrip-
        2. ⎨ tion of the problems, expert opinion, and au-
        3. ⎩ thoritative documentation.)
        4.

B. Expansion under the present system is not adequate for future needs.
1. Public needs
2. Private needs
3. Defense needs
C. While the need for adequate highways is apparent, the need for the federal government to develop an adequate highway program is the essence of the question under consideration. A main contention of the affirmative is that the present problems can be traced to a lack of federal development or, in short, to problems inherent within the status quo. Those problems are:
1. Interstate rivalry
2. Unequal distribution of wealth among the states
3. Much state road building is planned to satisfy short-range political objectives, rather than to carry out long-range interstate needs.

It should be noted that parts A and B in the example above are essentially expository. They describe a problem in the status quo. Part C is analytical, for it attempts to establish the reason for the existence of the problem. When both aspects of the need issue are established, they lead to the consideration of a solution. Attention now turns to the issues relevant to the solution.

Explaining the Issues Relevant to the Solution

Does the Affirmative Proposal Offer a Solution to the Problem? In school debating, the proposition itself states, in a more or less general way, the solution that is being advocated. The debate speaker must determine to what extent the solution ought to be enlarged and developed in order to form a clear plan of action. The practical question asked by the debater is, "How important is a well-defined plan?" The answer is that the importance varies. Essentially, the importance of the plan depends upon the nature of the problem. "Resolved: That capital punishment should be abolished" or "That the United States should resume diplomatic relations with Cuba" are examples of debate propositions for which detailed exposition of a plan of action is unnecessary. In these propositions, the plan is a procedural matter which may be regarded as not vital to the adoption of the proposal; the vital points concern the need for a change and the implications of change.

Other propositions advocate procedures which need to be clearly delineated. For example, in the question, "Resolved: That nuclear testing should be abolished," it is important to demonstrate that the procedure itself—a plan for the abolishment of nuclear testing—will work in a practical way to put the proposal into effect.

Many propositions call for the establishment of a new institution—a federal world government, permanent labor controls, or national health insurance. For each of these issues the affirmative speakers will be required to demonstrate, rather concretely, that their proposal will work in a practical way. Concreteness in the workability issue cannot be achieved without a tangible solution—a clear plan of action. This is not to say, however, that every detail of a plan needs to be discussed. The time limitations imposed on the debate speaker ought to suggest that such detail is not required.

The guiding principle here is that issues must be established, and the ability of the affirmative to establish the remaining issues depends to a large extent on the clarity with which the plan was presented. It is often overlooked that the most effective manner of proving a proposal is to apply it to the problem. If the proper application of solution (plan) to problem (need) is made, the demonstration itself is a persuasive argument for the adoption of the proposal. This type of application leads to a consideration of the other stock issues.

Is the Proposal Practical and Workable?   This element of the affirmative case, generally called the *workability issue*, often becomes the key issue in the debate. Depending on the nature of the proposition, the clash in the debate will usually center around the issue of need, the issue of workability, or on both of these vital points. While many affirmatives would like to be excused from the task of proving workability, it is nevertheless true that the advocate of change has a responsibility to establish the workability of the proposal.

The first responsibility of the advocate of change is to offer a solution that is practical. This simply means that the solution offered is not merely idealistic, but that it applies to normal human experience. Practicality is a vital point, for a proposal may satisfy all the other issues, yet be justifiably rejected on the basis of impracticality. For example, a proposal can be made both workable and beneficial by spending an exorbitant amount of money to make it so, but the basis of its workability may undermine its practicality. The general principle involved is that practicality must be judged in terms of its consistency with human experience.

Workability means that the affirmative speakers must prove that their solution really is a solution. A solution in debate is a proposal that will solve the problems upon which the need issue is based. If this application of solution to problem is not made, the affirmative is open to the charge of simply begging the question or arguing in a circle. Because this error is committed by so many debate speakers, the principle is emphasized here: A proposal cannot be justified because there is a need for a solution; a proposal can be justified only by demonstrating that it satisfies the need. The method used is to apply the solution to the problem.

Is the Proposal the Best Available Solution to the Problem? While this question usually does not emerge as a key issue in a debate, it is nevertheless vital in the process of analysis upon which the construction of the case depends. It bears directly on two aspects of the debate: (1) the plan of the affirmative and (2) the possible use of a counterplan by the negative.

The relevance of the question to the affirmative plan may be summarized by saying that, within the terms of the proposition, the affirmative faces the problem of tempering the desirability of its plan with practicality and workability. In short, the best plan may not be the one that seems to offer the most advantages, but the one which best balances the advantages and disadvantages.

This question suggests a second matter of concern—that there may be a solution to the affirmative need issue that is outside the terms of the proposition for debate. If this is so, the negative may offer that solution as a counterproposal. While the practice of offering counterproposals is somewhat unusual, it is nevertheless a part of debate and ought to be anticipated and prepared for by the affirmative speakers. As a general principle, do not be caught by surprise.

What Are the Implications of Adopting the Proposal? This question also bears directly on two aspects of the affirmative proposal—the possible disadvantages and the alleged advantages. The fact that both are important suggests that the affirmative speakers ought to consider all the possible implications of their proposal. To do so is, on the one hand, to prepare for negative objections which may arise and, on the other, to enhance the desirability of adopting the affirmative proposal.

Disadvantages. This aspect of the affirmative case is often called the issue of greater evils. It may emerge as a vital point in the debate because even if a solution is admitted to be workable, it may be justifiably rejected if it creates greater problems than it alleviates. The affirmative must anticipate negative arguments on disadvantages and be prepared either to demonstrate that the disadvantages will not occur or that they are more than balanced by the advantages to be gained.

Advantages. It is, of course, a benefit to solve the problems enumerated in the need issue. If the affirmative successfully applies its solution to the problems, then the enumeration of benefits becomes more than an exhortation based on question-begging assumptions. Persuasive appeal is given to the enumeration of benefits that actually emerge as concrete results of solving the problems. Furthermore, other benefits may emerge that are not directly related to the need issue. These may be called *added benefits* and ought to be considered. Indeed, in the absence of great disadvantages, added benefits constitute a kind of need in and of themselves. Debaters often overlook the persuasive appeal inherent in the exposition of reasonable benefits. The debate speaker should be reminded, however, that reasonable benefits emerge from the strength of the preceding issues. While the enumeration of benefits cannot give strength to a weak case, it can add to the effectiveness of a strong one. A special case may even be constructed out of compelling benefits, called the *comparative advantage approach.* In this case, the affirmative does not focus on needs or problems at all but simply on a new plan and the compelling advantages which they allege will result. In the comparative advantage approach, the benefits must still be sufficient and compelling to warrant a change in the present system. Whether you decide to use this method or simply to develop added benefits to a standard need-plan case, the general principle is the same: all implications of adopting the proposal ought to be considered.

Summary

The functions of the stock issues in the structure of a policy-oriented affirmative case are given in table 5.1. By keeping these stock issues in mind, you can question your case at each vital point in its development, and you can better question any opponents' cases once you understand how to do your own. Now let us turn to the analysis of an affirmative case and the stock issues in a value-oriented proposition.

Analyzing Value Propositions Through Stock Issues

Because debating about values in a school setting is relatively new, having begun with an association focus only in 1971, we do not enjoy a high level of universal agreement as to what constitutes stock issues in a value-oriented question. While others may phrase them in different ways, there seems to be relative agreement on several areas which we shall call stock issues. These issues can be analyzed through a question format much

Table 5.1
Summary: Analysis of Affirmative Case Structure

Stock Issues	Explanation	Questions to Be Asked in the Analysis and Refutation of Issues
I. Is there a need for a change from the present policy?	Since there are almost always some problems related to any policy or institution, this issue is generally the easiest to develop. The issue is hardly open to attack if the affirmative is allowed to base a need on the fact *that* problems exist. The *reason for* the problems is the essence of the affirmative need issue. The status of the issue is often one of quality: Is there enough of a need to justify a change?	Does the affirmative offer substantial evidence to indicate that problems exist? Does the affirmative make a fair analysis of the *status quo* with respect to all the available evidence? Does the affirmative relate the problems to inherent faults of the *status quo?* Do the problems enumerated constitute an adequate need for a change? Can the affirmative problems be solved within the *status quo?*
II. Does the affirmative proposal offer a solution?	The necessity of developing a concrete plan of action depends on the nature of the problem. The affirmative plan needs to be detailed enough so that its workability can be demonstrated.	Is the proposed plan consistent with the requirements of the proposition for debate, or does it limit the responsibility of the affirmative? Is the proposed plan consistent in itself? Does the solution suggest a clear plan of action, or is it vague?

III. Is the solution practical and workable?	A practical solution is one that is realistic in terms of human experience. The proof of workability is in the application of the affirmative proposal to the problems that constitute the need issue. This issue tends to become a question of quality: To what extent has the affirmative proved that its plan will work?	Has each point in the affirmative need issue been satisfied by the affirmative solution? Problems not solved cannot be fairly used as "needs." Is the proof of workability assumed, or is it demonstrated by evidence and reasoning? Is the solution realistic?
IV. Is the affirmative proposal the best solution available?	The problem of the affirmative is to temper the desirability of its solution with practicality and workability. The negative is justified in advocating a solution that is outside the terms of the proposition. This is called a counterproposal.	Does the proposition allow for a better solution? Is there a better solution available but not under the terms of the proposition for debate?
V. What are the implications of adopting the affirmative proposal?	The affirmative must consider all the implications of adopting the proposal, making certain that in solving some problems it does not create greater ones. If the affirmative has proved its case, benefits naturally result. The affirmative should also consider related benefits.	What are all the implications of adopting the proposed plan? Would the plan, in effect, cause other problems? Are the alleged benefits actually derived from adopting the proposal, or are these speculative and assumed benefits? Must the affirmative proposal be adopted to gain the benefits?

like that in the previous section. Remember that at the beginning, the affirmative must meet the issue of topicality before it can go on to any of the other stock issues.

Identifying the Value

Before beginning to write an affirmative case, you must decide what value or value system you will adopt and defend. Often, the phrasing of the resolution gives you the general perspective, such as "First Amendment rights are more important than any other Constitutional rights." Clearly, the affirmative must uphold the value of freedom of speech, religion, and the press, but they also need to explain why these are important. In order to do that, they will probably want to link those freedoms to other values, such as respect for human rights or even to the value of life itself.

Setting the Definition.   The affirmative would do well to define the terms of the resolution in accordance with recognized value systems or statements or authorities which clearly link the affirmative's interpretation of the question to a value system. If their definition is consistent with a value system related to authoritative discussion of the subject matter, then they will establish the topicality of the case.

Setting the Criteria.   The criteria are expressed early in the affirmative in order to establish a decision rule for the debate. The affirmative should suggest that the debate decision be awarded to the team which better upholds the dignity of the individual, national security, or some other defined value. If the affirmative does not specify a criteria for decision, the negative may offer their own.

Determining the Hierarchy.   Values, like policies, do not exist in a vacuum so much as they exist in a relationship. We offer exceptions to our values or describe circumstances where they would not apply. We often hold competing values and, thus, must assign them a priority relationship. This priority relationship is called a *hierarchy*. For example, we might think it a high value to help our friends when asked, but would not assist a friend in copying answers on a test because we value honesty above helping a friend cheat. Seemingly attractive values often conflict, and some value-oriented debates test that conflict through their subject matter, such as "Protection of the environment is more important than energy independence." Clearly, both positions could be supported by nearly everyone unless or until they are forced to choose between them. At this point a debate develops about value hierarchy. The affirmative must place its case in a hierarchy and compare it to any competing values mentioned in the proposition or any reasonably brought up against it by the negative.

Applying the Value

Linking It to the Status Quo. The affirmative needs to ask itself, "Is the value they are upholding a dominant value in current society, or should it be one?" The difference will help determine the presumption issue. If the affirmative can demonstrate that their value and its placement on society's hierarchy is consistent with the present system, then they may claim presumption. On the other hand, if such a claim is not easily made or readily apparent, then they need to establish that it ought to be incorporated by society or moved to a higher rank on the social value hierarchy.

Linking It to the Affirmative Case. Once the approach to the issue of presumption is determined by the affirmative, they then need to link their value to an affirmative case. They develop contentions which show the specific applications of the value to circumstances as they are or as they ought to be. The affirmative will likely spend the bulk of their time in the first affirmative constructive in this phase. They need to outline several areas of concern which demonstrate that the value they are defending is worth upholding and that support for the value meets the criteria for decision they put forth early in their presentation.

Developing Value Benefits. A third area you may develop would be the projection of any positive outcomes associated with adopting your value. For example, if new ways of evaluating the present system or even new beneficial policies or programs could be shown to result from your value structure, then you could claim value benefits. These value benefits, in themselves, can become a reason for the adoption of the affirmative case and certainly add an extra bonus to the affirmative position.

Impact of the Negative Case

This area of stock issue analysis asks the affirmative team to look at the potential areas of impact the opponents may develop against them and to construct a case so as to guard against these arguments. These areas will be further discussed in the section below on developing the negative case, but the wise affirmative will keep the possible negative issues in mind while constructing the affirmative. There are two major areas to think about.

Burden of Rejoinder. Initially in a debate, the negative will carry the burden of rejoinder—the duty to respond to the opposition. The affirmative might wish to play the role of a potential negative team while they are outlining their case to discover the immediately apparent responses. The affirmative can then construct their case so as to limit these responses, or they can develop potential answers for use as rebuttal material. These answers can be formalized as rebuttal sheets while the team prepares for tournament competition. For the time being, the affirmative needs to ask itself, "Are there readily obvious attacks on these ideas?" If so, then they need to proceed to the next question, "Can these obvious attacks be prevented by rewriting the case?" If so, then they should rewrite as necessary. If not, then they need to develop responses for use in rebuttal, or, if the attacks do not have a good defense, then the affirmative needs to consider reconstructing the entire case. Some affirmative teams have trouble admitting that their case has an easily attacked soft spot, or they may hope that their opposition will not discover their weak point. Championship affirmatives develop the ability to go beyond their ego involvement in a case and look at it objectively. They also realize that depending on the inability or ignorance of the opposition is a foolish and fatal wish. That attitude is like hoping no one else discovers a damaging piece of evidence which you have come across. Eventually, good research and good preparation will win out over wishes and hopes.

Significance of Value Objections. Value objections are similar in philosophy to the disadvantages offered against policy ideas. "What new problems or difficulties would be expected from the adoption of the affirmative position?" is the question each affirmative must ask itself at this point. Are there identifiable consequences flowing from the value advocated which could be significant enough to outweigh its possible good? If so, then the affirmative again needs to respond to these possibilities by rewriting its case, preparing for rebuttal, or selecting a new approach altogether. More will be said about value objections in the section on negative cases, but the vital questions about them must be considered by an affirmative during the construction of their case to save themselves significant problems later.

Burden of Communication

While certainly a concern for every speaker, whether in debate or in other situations, communication of ideas is a necessary burden for a debater dealing with value propositions. The debate ballot commonly used at value-oriented debate contests specifically lists the debaters' ability to communicate their ideas as an issue to vote upon. The founding of the Cross Examination Debate Association (*CEDA*) in 1971 was partly based on a desire to make school debating available to more general audiences. While many policy-oriented debaters certainly emphasize the amount and depth of their research, they too must be able to communicate the results of that research during a contest. A difference between the two types of debaters is that value-oriented debaters are expected to communicate their ideas and arguments at a tone and rate which a general audience of educated listeners could follow and respond to, while policy debaters are probably more concerned with reaching a specific audience of persons trained in debate theory and fully conversant with the debate topic under consideration. Thus, as they develop their case, value-oriented debaters on the affirmative need to ask themselves the question, "Am I communicating my ideas and arguments at a tone and rate which a general audience can follow and respond to?" If they try to use too many ideas, too many subpoints, or too many citations of evidence, they risk losing a general audience. The affirmative in this instance needs to edit material out of the case. They may do this by deleting multiple evidence for a single argument when one is sufficient to make the point, or they may wish to focus the case to fewer ideas and issues to that each may be developed as needed. Debaters are expected to present full evidence citation of their sources, and time must be allowed for that purpose during the presentation of the case. Attention to other factors of delivery will be covered in the chapter on presenting the debate.

You have seen how answering several standard questions, whether related to resolutions dealing with policy or value, can help you in building your affirmative case. In both situations, a general outline may be followed when you actually start to write your case.

Arranging the Affirmative Case

The process of putting the affirmative issues, arguments, and evidence together to make a persuasive debate speech will be treated in detail in chapter 8. At this point in the speakers' preparation, they should outline their case in three broad divisions: the introduction, body, and conclusion.

Introduction. The purpose of the introduction is to make the proposition clear and to prepare the way for the constructive arguments. An effective introduction has three parts:

1. An appropriate greeting, statement of the proposition, and definition of terms.

2. The statement of an affirmative philosophy, or general view, on the question. An effective statement of affirmative philosophy is based on an analysis which relates the affirmative proposition to the status quo and provides the affirmative speakers with the broadest possible basis of persuasive appeal. If debating a value-oriented proposition, you should also present your criteria for a decision rule in the debate round. This state-

ment aims to give perspective to the debate; it relates the proposition to the area of national or international concerns or values of which it is a subordinate part.

3. The preliminary outline, or preview, which provides an initial summary of the main affirmative contentions and serves as an effective transition to the main development of the case.

Body. The body is the main development of the affirmative issues, together with the supporting material. It will take up the largest amount of your time and should follow the numbering, sequence, and wording mentioned in the preview.

Conclusion. The conclusion should summarize the main contentions of the affirmative case and relate them to the proposition and the affirmative philosophy. When the conclusion is a succinct recapitulation of well-developed contentions stated in effective language, it should have a persuasive appeal in itself. Now that you have a start on constructing an affirmative case, it is time to briefly examine the negative.

Constructing the Negative Case

Since the methods for the analysis and support of the affirmative case also apply to the negative, the detailed exposition of stock issues, arguments, and evidence need not be repeated here. It should, however, be clear that those who speak against a proposed change of policy or against the adoption of a proposed value judgment have definite responsibilities in terms of the issues, the arguments, and the evidence.

In short, the purpose of the negative is to refute the case of the affirmative. The negative speakers may choose to use straight refutation, or to construct a case for the status quo, or to propose an alternative (a counterproposal) which is superior to that of the affirmative.

Straight Refutation

Straight refutation simply means a direct attack on the points of the affirmative case as presented. Depending on the phrasing of the topic and the affirmative's treatment of the issues, the negative may or may not base its refutation on defense of the status quo. For example, if a value-oriented resolution calls for the support of a new or existing secondary value over those currently in prominence, then a defense of current values would be called for and such a defense could form the core of a negative direct refutation. The negative dealing with a policy question would look at the affirmative's development of the need issue and decide whether a defense of status quo mechanisms pertaining to the need area would be their basis for refutation.

While it is technically correct that the negative is not obliged to develop a constructive defense of the status quo, the concept of straight refutation as a method distinct from the negative constructive case is somewhat misleading. The difference actually centers about the method of presentation for the negative arguments. The negative refutation may be presented either from the basis of the affirmative's case development (following the affirmative outline) or from the basis of a well-developed negative position on the proposition.

Since the affirmative cannot win its case without establishing *each* of its issues, the strategy of straight refutation is sometimes to devote the whole, or a great part, of the negative's time to the refutation of a single issue. The strategy may be effective, but it has the disadvantage of limiting the negative attack.

Most often, straight refutation is a point-by-point attack on the entire affirmative case. The advantage of this method is that it allows the negative speakers to present a great quantity of objections to the affirmative case and may give the negative an initial advantage that is difficult to overcome. There are at least three important disadvantages to the use of straight refutation as a method of procedure:

1. Straight refutation focuses attention on the affirmative case as presented. The method often fails to place the whole burden of proof on the affirmative because it takes advantage of only those negative arguments that apply directly to the particular affirmative case at hand. The negative may thus fail to consider the underlying generalizations so important to a full analysis of the affirmative. As we mentioned in the previous chapter, a

debate team which overlooks the opportunity to debate the underlying generalizations behind every argument, misses the essence of good, insightful debating.

2. The straight refutation of a poorly organized affirmative case tends to create a poorly organized negative. By simply adopting such an organization, the negative presentation will suffer from the faults of the affirmative.

3. Straight refutation often places the negative at a psychological disadvantage because people generally want the speaker to stand for something.

If you wish to use straight refutation, we suggest that you combine it with the ability to analyze the underlying generalizations, the strategy of spending greater or lesser time on affirmative arguments as they warrant, the willingness to modify organization to make it coherent, and the presentation of a clearly defined constructive argument favoring the negative position.

The Constructive Defense of the Status Quo

The constructive negative approach is based on the idea that general analysis of the resolution will yield certain fundamentally strong negative positions on the issues and that these negative positions ought to be introduced into the debate as constructive arguments. The method helps to make the negative position clear, and it may place an additional burden of refutation on the affirmative. The method is based on a complete analysis of the present system (its policies or values) and results in a negative approach to the proposition that is analytic in nature. It focuses attention on the strongest aspects of the status quo and places the full burden of proof on those who advocate change. The constructive defense of the status quo may admit some faults while supporting the position that these faults can best be corrected by modification of the status quo (policy), or that the faults are outweighed by the strengths of the status quo (value), rather than by adopting the affirmative proposal.

The affirmative case, it should be said, is not ignored by a constructive negative. Rather, a constructive negative ought to facilitate refutation by allowing the negative to refute affirmative arguments within the context of a clearly developed negative position. The result should be a direct clash of affirmative analysis on the issues versus negative analysis of the issues. This clash is the aim of the constructive negative position. If it is even partially accomplished, it is clearly preferable to a straight enumeration of unrelated objections. The negative constructive allows the negative to develop a consistent philosophy; a coherent structure of preplanned issues, arguments, and evidence; and its own ground to support throughout the debate.

The Counterproposal and Counterwarrant

The negative may refute the affirmative policy position by admitting the need issue and offering a solution which is not possible under the terms of the affirmative's proposition. This negative strategy is called a *counterproposal* and includes an attack on the affirmative plan. It requires the negative to accept an equal burden of proof to demonstrate that its plan is practical, workable, and more desirable than the affirmative proposal. In a value topic debate, the negative may develop competing values not called for in the resolution and attempt to show that these new values should replace the ones advocated by the affirmative. This negative strategy is called a *counterwarrant*. In both situations, the obligations placed upon the negative, as well as questions in the minds of some judges about the very legitimacy of the approach, make these options unusual and risky, especially for any but the very experienced debater. Our advice is to combine a defense of the status quo with judicious refutation of key affirmative issues, either by presenting them in both of the negative speeches or by having one negative speaker concentrate on the negative constructive while the other works primarily on refutation of the affirmative.

Arranging the Negative Case

As in the affirmative, a three part construction will help you to remember what to do as you approach the negative case.

Introduction. The purpose of the introduction for the negative team is to make their initial position clear and to set up the arguments to be offered by the team. It will likely have three main aspects:

1. An appropriate greeting, restatement of the proposition, and comment or reaction or response to the definition of terms.

2. The statement of a negative philosophy, or general view, on the proposition. In value-oriented debate, this section should also respond to the criteria, if offered, and provide a negative perspective to the debate. As with the affirmative, this statement should relate the negative position to the values, attitudes, or policies of the status quo and provide them with the broadest possible basis of persuasive appeal.

3. The preliminary outline, or preview, of the division of labor which the negative will employ—which speaker will concentrate specifically on which issues—and an initial summary of the main negative contentions in brief form.

Body. This section provides the main development of the negative issues and may be divided into two subsections. The first subsection may consist of supporting the status quo through negative contentions, while the second subsection may deal with straight refutation of selected parts of the affirmative case.

Conclusion. The conclusion should summarize the negative position on the definitions (and criteria if in a value-oriented debate), the negative philosophy, negative contentions (if used), and the negative position on affirmative contentions or issues. If this material is communicated in a succinct, well-organized manner, it may create an impression of a large barrier for the affirmative to overcome and thus, will be very persuasive to the audience.

This chapter looked at ways to begin your construction of affirmative and negative cases and introduced you to the concepts of planning for refutation as well as for defense of your arguments. Once you have begun outlines for your affirmative and negative positions, you should review each of the questions mentioned and test your case against them. You will then be ready to consider, in depth, how to refute another's case—which is the subject of the next chapter.

6

Refutation

Refutation is the key element in debate and makes the whole process exciting by relating ideas and arguments from one team to those of the other. It is challenging because it is more spontaneous than reading prepared speeches. Refutation is based on good research, good constructive development, and good anticipation of potential attacks. It is the essence of debate and is difficult to master. A great deal of practice and attention to the basic principles outlined in this chapter will help guide you to becoming an effective debater through skillful refutation.

Indirect and Direct Refutation

Considerable confusion has centered about the term *refutation* because it is a broad term that is usually given a narrow application. The end, or purpose, of refutation is implicit in its definition: refutation is the attempt to demonstrate the error or inadequacy of the opponents' case. It is clear that the end of refutation is to destroy; the means used may be indirect or direct. Because debate is a unified process of persuasion, you can see that refutation occurs indirectly in constructive arguments, and that it occurs directly as the responsibility of meeting particular arguments shifts from the negative back to the affirmative.

Indirect

Debaters refute through an indirect means when they use counterargument to attack the case of the opponent. Counterargument is the demonstration of such a high degree of probability for your conclusions that the opposing view loses its probability and is rejected. For example, the affirmative need issue may be supported by arguments A, B, and C. Negative refutation of the need issue may be the development of arguments X, Y, and Z. Although the refutation for the argument is indirect, there is a direct clash on the need issue. The use of counter argument is the strategy of the constructive negative case.

Direct

Direct refutation attacks the arguments of the opponent with no reference to the constructive development of an opposing view. For example, it attacks the affirmative need issue by demonstrating the error or inadequacy of arguments A, B, and C. The most effective refutation, as you can probably guess, is a combination of the two methods so that the strengths of the attack come from both the destruction of the opponents' views and the construction of an opposing view.

To conceive refutation broadly, think of the affirmative case as the refutation of the status quo and the constructive negative case as refutation of the affirmative. While you may think of a constructive case apart from the idea of refutation, remember that constructive argument develops largely from counterargument. There is, however, a difference between the presentation of constructive arguments and the presentation of arguments intended to apply directly to the particular arguments of the opponent. The former is part of that broad look at refutation and may be developed in advance of the debate through your analysis of potential opposing arguments. Because the latter task is done largely during the debate, it is one of the most complex the debate speaker encounters. It is the aspect of debating that is most often done poorly. In the process of debate there is a confrontation of the affirmative and the negative views. This may easily be viewed as a confrontation between opposing outlines. In this process, direct refutation is an important means of attack.

Using Refutation Effectively

We have just emphasized that refutation has both a constructive and a destructive means, and that while the purpose of refutation may be accomplished by either, it is most effectively accomplished by using both. It should be added that refutation and rebuttal, attack and defense, are opposite sides of the same coin and that the methods used apply to both. Direct refutation demonstrates the error or inadequacy of the opponents' case, while defense demonstrates the error or inadequacy of the opponents' refutation. In both cases, the debate speaker's method is the same—building the refutation and rebuttal on the analysis of the reasoning process and evaluation of evidence. Let us now focus on direct refutation, the destructive means of defeating the opponents' case.

Methods of Direct Refutation

To refute the case of an opponent is to demonstrate the error or inadequacy of the arguments upon which it is based. Because arguments are the result of reasoning about evidence, the two kinds of direct refutation are attacks on the evidence itself and attacks on reasoning (the meaning of evidence).

Attacks on Evidence

Since refutation aims to demonstrate error or inadequacy, the two broad tests of evidence are: Is the evidence correct? and Is the evidence adequate to prove the argument? The following questions are offered as more particular criteria for testing evidence.

Testing the Facts:

1. Are the facts presented consistent in themselves?
2. Are the facts consistent with other known facts, or does the evidence appear as unusual, picked evidence?
3. Are enough facts introduced to support the conclusions derived from them?
4. Are the facts accurate as they are presented?
5. Are the facts verified with good supporting documentation, and is the source used qualified to know and report the facts?

Testing the Opinion:

1. Is the opinion from a qualified source? Is the source an expert in the subject under consideration? Is the source prejudiced? Is this expert usually accurate?
2. Does the quotation cited give a fair indication of the person's real opinion, or was it lifted from context or otherwise distorted?
3. Is the opinion consistent with other assertions the authority has made?
4. What is the reason for the authority's opinion? Opinions are based upon reasoning and are subject to the same tests of reasoning which apply elsewhere.

In summary, the refutation of evidence is limited to the questions of correctness and the adequacy of the evidence. An idea that needs to be stressed is that merely matching sets of evidence does not result in good debating. In our opinion, the most common fault of debate speakers on all levels is that they are too often content to limit their refutation to a matching of evidence. For example, in a debate on the policy question of adopting a federal program of health insurance, the affirmative might argue that there is a need for compulsory health insurance and support this argument with evidence showing that in cities A and B, a significant percentage of the aged receive inadequate medical care. The negative might respond with evidence which indicates that in cities C and D the aged are well cared for and, thus, no need exists. This futile matching of evidence results in an unfounded leap from the evidence to the issue. Argument, or reasoning about the meaning of evidence, is omitted. If reasoning is omitted from debate, and if analysis is lost in simply comparing different piles of note cards, then school debate is guilty of poor education as charged by its critics. The proper relationship of the evidence would suggest that some problems do exist, and subsequent reasoning ought to be along the lines of finding out whether enough problems exist to constitute a need, whether the problems are inherent within the status quo, and ultimately, whether the affirmative provides an adequate solution to the problems.

When a *New York Times* reporter assigned to the United States Supreme Court was asked to evaluate the debating done at a national debate tournament, his criticism was that the debaters tended merely to match evidence, not bothering to discuss the implications of the evidence. He suggested, not completely in jest, that the debaters simply matched cards on each side of the resolution until one side ran out of evidence, and thus lost the debate.

Evidence, of course, is absolutely vital to debate because it is the foundation upon which logical argument is based. But, on any debatable issue, there will be a wealth of evidence on each side. Matching evidence does not constitute good debating. Reasoning about the meaning of the evidence and the meaning of conflicting evidence, on the other hand, can result in debate speaking which has genuine analytic value. That is why it is still possible to debate an opponent's argument even when you may not have any specific evidence yourself. You can very legitimately analyze and attack the faults and errors of the conclusions which the opponents have reasoned from their evidence. Often, the very strongest debating is done, not about the evidence, but about the links, correlations, connections, and implications of the evidence.

Attacks on Reasoning

In good debate, the evidence is usually not questionable, the facts are as the speakers say they are, the opinions cited are those of recognized authorities, and each debater has a thorough knowledge of the evidence. Conflict, therefore, should center on the meaning of the evidence and on reasoning about the facts and opinions.

Since argument in debate is nothing more than the oral expression which results from the process of reasoning, any debate speaker must develop skill in talking about the process by which conclusions are derived from evidence. In short, the question is, "How does one talk about reasoning?" To answer this question, one must return to concepts introduced in the previous chapter. If reasoning can be described according to the relationship of the evidence to the conclusion, then the correctness of arguments ought to be measured by questions which test the correctness of that relationship. Table 6.1 is provided as a guide to the testing of arguments. In using the table, the reader should recall the guiding principle underlying all tests of argument— that every argument is either based on a generalization (deductive) or makes a generalization (inductive).

Applying the Tests of Argument

The foregoing materials demonstrate that the refutation of argument depends on analysis of the reasoning process. Debaters ought to apply the tests of argument to their own cases and make whatever further study they can of the process of argumentation. We strongly urge you to follow up with advanced readings in this area or even courses in argumentation, debate, critical thinking, or logic.

Three Common Errors in Reasoning

Before leaving the analysis of argument, the debater's attention should be directed to three fallacies, or errors, in reasoning, which often occur in school debating. These are the fallacies of question begging, of extension, and of hasty generalization. While there are other fallacies, some of which are special sub-units of these three, we believe that understanding these major errors will help get you started right away in building good reasoning skills and, later, prepare you to understand and avoid the others.

Question Begging

The error of the question-begging argument is that it assumes the essential point that it ought to prove. For example, Jo argues that engineering students should not have to waste their time taking liberal arts courses. It may be agreed that engineering students (or any students) ought not waste their time, but the essential point to be established with reasoning and evidence is that liberal arts courses are a waste of time for engineering students. Beware of the unsupported assumption.

Furthermore, the question-begging error may pertain to the whole case. Many debate teachers are alarmed by how frequently they encounter an affirmative case which is based on question begging. In practice, the erroneous reasoning goes like this:

1. Problems exist which constitute a need for change.
2. Therefore, the affirmative proposal should be adopted.
   OR
1. The values of the current system have faults.
2. Therefore, the resolution ought to be upheld.

The unsupported assumption here is that the affirmative case will solve the problems or respond to the faults. The workability or desirability of the affirmative cannot simply be assumed without begging the question. A similar error is called the *post hoc fallacy* and assumes that because one event follows another, the first one caused the second. An example would be a debater presenting evidence showing a decline in unemployment after the institution of a federal program and then assuming that the program was responsible for the decline. Unless some direct link is demonstrated, the mere sequence of events is not enough to support the conclusion. These two problems both stem from faulty assumptions which imply or presume a relationship that may not exist.

Extension

This error occurs when the debater either exaggerates the meaning of evidence in order to make it prove more than it actually should or when the debater exaggerates the opponents' position in order to make it easier to attack. The error is avoided by learning to use evidence judiciously and by developing a sense of fairness and objectivity in dealing with the argument of the opponent. Many debaters get used to thinking about ideas, issues, arguments, and even evidence in a standard way and often miss the meaning of an opponent who offers a similar idea, but with a unique slant. The debater who is not listening carefully then attacks an argument that was expected, but not the one actually presented. If you hear a negative speaker claiming, "This affirmative team would support greater freedom of information, thus making birth control materials easily available to high school students and destroying the American family," you are witnessing an error in extension. Concentration, good note taking, and listening skills will help you avoid this embarrassing error, and thus help you avoid the fallacy of extension.

Hasty Generalization

A hasty generalization is the drawing of a conclusion about a group of instances when not enough of the instances have been observed. For example, if a speaker were to read a quotation which indicates that the public schools in Detroit have a 45% drop out rate and then conclude that "education in the United States is failing," you could easily see that this limited, and probably special, example does not provide enough information to support the generalization. The example would need to be combined with some sort of national statistic to avoid the fallacy. Debate speakers who seek the dramatic appeal of broad, sweeping assertions are most liable to stumble over their hasty generalizations. Debaters who realize that they are dealing with probabilities and approach their subject reasonably and judiciously, will take the time to establish dependable generalizations.

Summary of Principles in Direct Refutation

Direct refutation attacks the opponent's arguments and evidence to demonstrate the error or inadequacy. This attack is made in three general ways:

1. Demonstrating error by showing that the alleged facts or opinions either are not true, or, if true, are irrelevant.

2. Demonstrating error by showing that even if the evidence is accurate and relevant, the conclusions drawn are not correct.

3. Demonstrating inadequacy by showing that even if the evidence is acceptable, it is, nevertheless, insufficient to warrant the conclusions drawn; or, that even if the arguments are justified, they are insufficient to establish the issues.

Organization of Refutation

The Overall Organization

Where should refutation be placed so that it will most effectively attack the opponents' arguments and ensure a direct clash in the debate? In answer, it should be said that clash will occur naturally in those debates where both sides have carefully analyzed the issues and developed arguments in support of their positions.

This is not to say, however, that either the second affirmative speaker or the negative speakers can read or memorize a pat speech. In the first place, all these speakers need to be versatile enough to avoid spending time on arguments that may already have been conceded. But, most importantly, as the constructive arguments of the negative are developed, their relationship to the affirmative case should be clarified. The method is to present the constructive argument, and immediately to show the effect of the argument on the affirmative constructive case. This is effective refutation within the context of negative constructive

arguments. The second affirmative speaker has the same obligation—to complete the construction of the affirmative case and,
at the same time, to relate that case to the attack of the opposition. The most effective method is to answer the negative attack
within the context of the affirmative case structure. The debate
speaker who develops skill in this method will find that refutation will spring from strength.

Example: Refutation
Here is a sample of what a negative speaker might say in refutation to the need issue of an affirmative case calling for a policy of
permanent price controls. Note how the speaker incorporates
many ideas and their relationship and impact with an economy
of words.

"So, in summary, the negative has admitted that some problems could exist because of fluctuations in prices, but we have
developed the contention that these problems do not constitute
a need for the federal government to adopt a plan of permanent
legislation to control prices. The negative reasoning has been
based on the fact that there are now twenty-one state laws to
control prices, in addition to ten federal agencies with price-
setting authority. With this permanent legislation already a part
of the status quo, the affirmative is faced with two obligations:
(1) to demonstrate what is inherently wrong with the thirty-one
controls now in operation; and (2) of greater significance, the
affirmative needs to trace the present problems to a lack of permanent controls, because it seems apparent that the problems
enumerated by the affirmative are not owing to a lack of legislation. In short, the affirmative simply offers one more law to add
to the thirty-one now in operation. They must demonstrate why
this one will work."

What should the affirmative response be at this point? Do
they give up and admit defeat? We hope not! Instead, the affirmative should adapt to the negative attack. If the above negative
refutation occured in the first negative constructive, it should be

answered when it becomes relevant to the second affirmative speech. In this case, it would be relevant to the affirmative plan and its workability. The affirmative might say something like what follows.

"Before we proceed to the defense of the affirmative plan and its workability, remember that the negative has admitted that problems exist in the present system that ought to be solved. Their position is that future legislation will not be effective and should not even be tried because past legislation, which they defend, has failed. The negative position is defeatism, and if we all adopted their philosophy, progress would halt. However, the important idea for you to remember about the affirmative is that our proposal is better than any previous legislation, and it will work to solve those problems that both teams agree exist in the present system. Let me now turn to the plan and show you how it is superior and, thus, how it answers the negative attack."

As you can see, the affirmative speaker has accepted the challenge of the negative in a confident manner and has previewed how that challenge will be answered. Notice that the speaker answers from the perspective of the affirmative case and concludes on affirmative ground. The speaker will now proceed to show how the plan will work to solve the problems and why it will work where others have failed. Well-prepared speakers will meet the opponents' objections by returning to their own case, their own ground.

It is easier for a speaker to return to and defend an argument or the entire case if the debate has developed from two opposing outlines. Keep your own outline in mind as you compare and contrast it to the outline of your opponents.

In short, the effect of placing one constructive case outline against another avoids the pitfalls of matching evidence but may result in the matching of constructive arguments. It may be argued that even this result is far more desirable than matching evidence. It should still be emphasized that the superior debate will not only demonstrate the clash of a clearly defined affirmative position versus a clearly defined negative position but there will also be an analysis of the relationship of these two positions. Arguments will be related to those of the opposition so that the effect of one argument on another will be clarified. The results to be expected would include smaller areas of difference between the two sides, greater clarification of the key arguments upon which the issues turn, and the debate as a whole would tend toward a more rational approach to deciding questions than the right versus wrong often heard when an affirmative opposes a negative.

Organizing Particular Arguments

Whether in the constructive speeches or in the rebuttal period, the debate speaker ought to view the whole case of the opponents and evaluate the effect of the total attack. Nevertheless, as the speakers talk about the attack of the opposition, they must limit the refutation to one argument at a time. While preceding paragraphs have stressed the importance of relating the particular refutation to the whole case, the intention here is to offer a guide to the refutation of particular arguments. There are five steps in the process of refuting an argument effectively.

Five Steps in Refutation

1. State with absolute clarity what it is you are going to refute.
2. Clarify the relationship of the argument to be refuted to the attack of the opponent.
3. State how you will refute the argument.
4. Present your argument in refutation.
5. Indicate the effect of your refutation on the issue in question and relate the effect to its impact on the opponents' case.

In print, these five steps may seem to be cumbersome, but in practice they are completed briefly with the use of effective language. The refutation given in the following example can be completed in less than one minute.

Example: Five Steps in Refutation

STEPS 1 AND 2:
The argument to be refuted and its relationship to the case as a whole.

STEP 3:
How it will be refuted.

STEP 4:
Refutation with supporting evidence.

STEP 5:
The effect of the refutation.

Transition to continued refutation.

In developing a need for price controls, the affirmative has argued that the effect of inflation has been injurious to the welfare of the American laborer. Now, if this were true, the affirmative would indeed have a strong argument. However, it can be demonstrated that the affirmative has reached an erroneous conclusion by neglecting the most relevant aspects of the United States economic picture. Has the United States laborer been hurt by inflation? On the contrary, according to the Secretary of the Treasury, his buying power has gone up forty per cent in the past twenty years, and according to a study conducted by the labor organizations themselves (AFL-CIO report), "The laborer, even though prices have gone up, still is in a position to buy more of the desired goods on the market than ever before." Thus we see that the affirmative need argument, an appeal to the welfare of labor, is refuted by the labor leaders themselves. Now, let us proceed to their other need arguments to see if they are real or largely imaginary.

Language of Refutation

Because refutation is always concerned with the communication of rather complex ideas, it is highly important that the debater make the means of communication—language—as clear as possible. Avoid vague terms and use the vocabulary of debate by referring to issues, arguments, and evidence. If the opponents have labeled an argument a certain way, use the same label when referring to it. Likewise, in your own case, use consistent references to your ideas and outline in all your speeches. This care is not always evident, as the forms in table 6.2 indicate. These examples were taken directly from college debate speakers in a tournament situation.

Seven Guiding Principles for Refutation

1. The most effective refutation is from a strong constructive case.

2. Evidence is refuted by testing its correctness and its adequacy as used.

3. Arguments are refuted by attacking their basis of support—evidence—and by attacking the reasoning—the relationship of the evidence to the conclusion.

4. Debate speakers must relate their arguments to those of their opponents in order to demonstrate the effect of the refutation.

5. The effect of refutation must be related to its impact on the debate as a whole. This relationship has three implications: (1) the refutation of evidence is related to invalidating or weakening arguments which that evidence tries to support; (2) the refutation of arguments aims at resolving the issues of the debate in your favor; and (3) the loss of a single issue results in the defeat of the affirmative case.

6. Refutation must be clearly organized to be effective. Follow the five-step process outlined above for each and every idea you refute.

Table 6.1
Summary: Analysis of Argument

Kind of Argument	Explanation	Example	Tests
Sign	The argument asserts that the presence of A indicates the presence of B.	A build-up of troops in North Korea indicates hostile intentions toward South Korea.	Is the sign adequate to prove the conclusion, or are there other signs necessary for corroboration? (The probability of an argument from sign is strengthened as additional signs are introduced to support the conclusion.) Have unusual circumstances occurred which change the normal sign relationships? (The build-up of troops may be relevant to the internal affairs of North Korea, or South Korea may have staged a troop build-up first.)
Causal	The argument asserts that if fact A exists, it will cause fact B to follow. Or, in past fact, A was followed by B; therefore, A was the cause of B.	Future fact: The invasion of South Korea would lead to a general war in Asia. Past Fact: During the past three Democratic administrations there have been	Is the cause adequate to produce the alleged effect? Will other factors alter the alleged cause-effect relationship? In past fact, is the cause di-

	Description	Example	Questions/Tests
		wars. Therefore, Democratic administrations cause wars.	rectly related to the alleged effect, or could there have been other causes for the same effect?
Analogous	The argument asserts that if facts relating to A and facts relating to B are alike in some essential respects, they will be alike in another, or other, essential respects.	The war in South Korea was fought as a limited war with characteristics A, B, and C; so it follows that a war in Laos would also exhibit characteristics A, B, and C.	Are the cases really alike in essential respects? Are enough comparisons made to support the probability of the conclusion?
Example	This is the inductive form of reasoning that provides the generalizations upon which deductive argument is based.	A build-up of troops in Vietnam, Burma, North Korea, and Laos each led to war; therefore, all such cases of troop build-ups leads to war.	Are enough examples given to justify the generalization that is made? Are the examples clearly related to the generalization? (Are the examples really instances of the circumstances being generalized?)

Table 6.2
The Language of Refutation

Avoid these expressions:	*Because:*	*Use instead:*
"The point has been brought up"	Vague. Calling everything a point, whether it is an issue, an argument, or evidence, is probably the most common language error in debate. By itself it is vague; when it is overused it leads to total confusion.	"The contention of workability has been attacked with the argument that"
"As our quotes have proved"	Vague. Be concrete by making specific references.	"On the other hand, both Professor X, of White University, and the Director of the National Science Foundation have"
"They said" or "We said"	Vague and clumsy.	"The first affirmative speaker asserted" or "Miss Smith, in her first constructive speech" or "The contention has been"

"The negative hasn't had too much evidence to support"	Clumsy. This use of too is sometimes called the "too tautology." Not only does it beg the question of how much evidence is enough, but it negates a circumstance that probably could not exist. Could the negative have too much supporting evidence?	"The negative has offered insufficient evidence to support"
"The status quo is taking care of" or "Our plan takes care of that"	Trite.	"The problems are being effectively solved within the status quo" or "Those problems would be solved if the affirmative were adopted, for"
"There is no need"	Trite. The more judicious approach is probably that the need is insufficient, not that there is no need whatsoever.	"While the negative will quickly admit that there are some problems in our contemporary society, the negative view is that these problems can

Avoid these expressions:	Because:	Use instead:
		best be solved within the framework of the status quo, and do not constitute a need for a major policy change."
"The opposition's contention does not stand up"	Trite.	"The contention of the affirmative has not been adequately supported" or "The contention has, therefore, been defeated"
"During my partner's stand on the floor"	Trite and clumsy.	"During the first negative speech" or "During the constructive speech of my colleague"
"They came back and said"	Clumsy.	"The negative's response was"

"How did they hit this?"	Clumsy, although the use of a question to clarify and emphasize is effective.	"What was the attack on this argument?" or "Let me call your attention to the manner in which this argument was refuted."
"The members of the opposition brought forth the argument"	Clumsy; at best archaic.	"The opposition introduced the argument"
"We stand on"	Clumsy.	"Our support for this contention has been"
"We backed this up"	Clumsy.	"We supported"
"Where is their proof?" and "We have offered proof"	Clumsy and erroneous. Proof is often confused with evidence.	"Where is the supporting evidence to prove" "We have offered evidence to support"

7. The language of refutation must be clear, concise, and direct. Avoid the common errors outlined in table 6.2, even though you may hear them used by others.

This chapter was designed to show how to attack the opponents' case through refutation. One of the ways to discover potential areas for attack is by asking your opponent questions about their case. That process of asking questions is called cross-examination and is the subject of the next chapter.

7

Introduction to Cross-Examination

Before presenting specific guidelines for doing cross-examination, we will define and describe cross-examination as it is used in the school debate setting.

Cross-examination may be defined as the purposeful asking and answering of questions about the issues in the debate during an established time format. An effective cross-examination will consist of a series of carefully worded questions which establish an order, or a sequence, of ideas which help to persuade the audience that you and your statements are worthy of belief.

Cross-examination was present at many high school tournaments, but was relatively rare in college debating until the mid-1970s, when the Cross Examination Debate Association (CEDA) was formed and began to sponsor a nationwide series of debate tournaments featuring a cross-examination format. The National Debate Tournament (*NDT*) then adopted a cross-examination format for its tournament, and, shortly thereafter, cross-examination became a standard feature at virtually every high school and college debate tournament. While it may have some resemblance to the cross-examination done in the court-room, it does have its own goals, rules, and regulations.

Goal

The primary goal of cross-examination is to persuade the audience to accept your position and reject that of your opponents. You can reach this goal through the purposeful asking of a series of questions designed to lead the respondent into statements or admissions which will have a persuasive effect on the audience. There are four means to accomplish the goal of cross-examination, and these pertain to both the person asking the questions (examiner) and the person responding to the questions (respondent). These means are to build your own credibility, to clarify issues in your opponents' case, to expose possible weaknesses in the opponents' case, and to build your skills of focusing on issues and responding to questions. Let us go through these areas one at a time and see how you can meet them.

Building Credibility

You must be believed by your audience if you are to be an effective debater. Aristotle identified this aspect of communication over two thousand years ago and called it *ethos*. By this he meant the way an audience perceives the speaker's character. In modern times, research has consistently identified four factors which influence the audience's perception of a speaker's credibility. These factors are dynamism, expertise, trustworthiness, and goodwill.

Dynamism.   An audience will find you dynamic if you ask and answer questions in a positive, assertive tone. You should maintain good eye contact with your opponent and your audience. You should stand near the center of the speaking area when you are asking and answering questions, and use good techniques of facial expression and gesture as you would in any speaking situation. When you are listening to questions, or to answers to your questions, you should remain courteous and respectful.

Expertise.   To create a favorable impression of expertise, you should ask questions which reveal a thorough knowledge of the topic and which are directly related to the opponents' case.

Likewise, your answers should show that you understand the topic and have specific supporting material for your responses.

Trustworthiness. Trustworthiness will be communicated by being consistent in your questions and answers. You cannot change your case or your issues to avoid answering a tough question. The material you present in cross-examination should be of the same high quality as the material you would present in your constructives. If you do not know the answer, it is better honestly to admit it than to try to bluff your way with a low-quality answer. You can always offer to try to respond during your subsequent speech (but remember, you then must fulfill your promise or you greatly diminish your trustworthiness).

Goodwill. Finally, goodwill can be demonstrated by both examiner and respondent by keeping the exchange at a friendly, professional, and issue-oriented tone. Good humor is appropriate, sarcasm and personal attack are not. Many debaters lose considerable impact (and thus points and possibly even the debate) because they do not distinguish between what they consider humor and what the audience perceives as rudeness. Goodwill is especially important when two teams are clearly at different skill levels. The more advanced team must make certain to remain professional and not fall into a superior or condescending style.

If you keep in mind the requirements for building good ethos, or strong credibility, everything else you say in the debate will likely have greater impact. Likewise, poor performance during the cross-examination can damage your impact in the rest of the debate.

Clarifying Issues of the Opponents' Case

The time for cross-examination is meant for you, as examiner, to clear up any possible areas of misunderstanding. Suppose you did not get a source citation for a key piece of evidence the opposition has offered, cross-examination is the time to get that citation so that you may then evaluate it according to the tests of evidence. Likewise, you may have careful notes, but they indicate no evidence supporting an argument of the opposition. In cross-examination you can ask, "Did you have any supporting material for your argument concerning the growth of energy conservation—contention II., section C?" If they did, and you missed it, then you can avoid the embarrassment of saying later, "They offered no support for this argument!" when the judge and audience all remember that they did. Be careful in cross-examination, however, that you simply do not ask the opponents to reread or re-explain major sections of their case which you should have gotten the first time. Asking for repetition of an idea or phrase should be done sparingly as a beginner and probably not at all when you become accomplished at listening and note taking during a debate.

It is important to emphasize that the cross-examination period is for the examiner to focus on the case of the respondent. It is not the time to offer extensions of your arguments which you forgot during your speech, it is not the time to bring up evidence they asked for previously, and it is not the time for you to argue with your opponent over issues. It is the time to clarify the issues of the case, to proceed with analysis, and to probe the opponents' case for weakness.

Exposing Potential Weaknesses in the Opponents' Case

This aspect may be the most exciting part of the cross-examination period. You can ask opponents to defend or justify their philosophy, their definitions, their case area and focus, their limitation of issues, their selection of arguments, their reasoning in drawing conclusions and connections, and their use of evidence. Again, let us emphasize that your purpose is not to expose your opponents' personal weaknesses, but the weaknesses in their case. It takes some skill and tact to avoid crossing the line between attack of ideas and attack of persons. This skill may be hard for beginning debaters, but we have seen advanced speakers who cross over this line as well. An easy way to remind yourself of the proper focus is to begin each question with a reference to a specific item or place in the opposing case, something like: "I want to ask about the first contention where you cite a twenty-year-old study to support your argument about new developments in technology. Given the rapid advancement in the technical fields, how do you justify supporting your argument with this evidence?" Such a question focuses on the analytical aspect of the use of evidence and really places a burden on the respondent without resorting to sarcasm, such as: "How can you be so foolish as to use such crummy evidence! That mistake gives us the round." Such statements are to be avoided because they are more a personal observation than a probe of the opponents' analysis.

Another kind of question to avoid is the question which makes it sound like *you* are the confused person. For example, "I don't understand your use of evidence in contention II. B." This is really a statement about your own inability rather than a challenge for them to defend their case. Such beginnings as "I don't see . . . ," "I don't understand . . . ," or "I'm confused about . . ." damage your own ethos either by making yourself appear weak or by being interpreted as sarcasm. Ask straightforward questions linked to an aspect of the oppositions' case.

Developing the Ability to Focus and Respond

These two skills are important in both roles of asking questions and answering them. When you are the examiner, plan carefully so you can ask precise questions. When you have only three minutes to accomplish your cross-examination, it becomes very important to be concise about phrasing your ideas. You might remember the examples above which begin with a reference to a specific aspect of the opponents' case. Avoid extraneous verbiage such as, "Umm, okay, let's see now." Your cross-examination time is precious. Work for economy in language, and try something like: "We question your conclusion on contention II. A, where you attempt to justify a 1,000 percent increase in taxes. Please explain how you arrived at the figure and indicate what evidence or analysis supports it." This phrasing is direct, concise, and specific in its requirements of the respondent.

Stay away from negative questions ("Don't you agree that there is not enough energy in the United States?" or "Aren't your studies old?"). These questions are also rhetorical, meaning that the answer is implied in the sentence, and they are really more like statements than questions. The faults of negative and rhetorical questions are to be avoided.

When you are the respondent, try to be concise and direct in your answers. Some examiners will badger an opponent by insisting they answer yes or no to a very complex or overly simplified question. If you can honestly answer yes or no, do so. If you cannot, say so and tell why. The respondent will not help build ethos by being deliberately evasive.

If the question is obviously relevant, answer it with the same skills you would use to question an opponent. If the question is open-ended, such as, "Please explain your case," then the fault is in the question, and you may feel free to summarize your entire case from introduction onward. However, do not try to dodge a question in anticipation of how it will be used. Answer simply and directly and from your own ground. We will now take a look at the types of questions which are asked in cross-examination.

Types of Questions

There are four primary types of questions you will want to use. They are direct, open, probe, and leading questions.

Direct

Direct questions are those which refer to a specific piece of information and usually have a short answer. Such questions as, "What was the source for your definition of energy?" or "Do you support mandatory penalties for violations of your plan?" are examples of direct questions.

Open

Open questions allow the respondent to amplify ideas and probably should be limited to explanations of implications of the case, rather than repetitions of ideas already presented. Saying, "Tell us why you favor mandatory execution of violators" is better than "Explain your plan's philosophy." The respondent can then amplify and perhaps even reveal information which will help you to develop a response later.

Probe

Probe questions are similar to open questions in requiring a longer answer than direct ones, but they are more limited than open questions. They are often directed at a specific line of reasoning which the opponents have used. For example, you can ask an opponent, "Why does the affirmative depend exclusively on federal government sources to support the need for federal intervention?" Such a question might reveal weakness in the research base of the affirmative or lead to the development of a negative attack concerning bias in evidence. Trying to delve beneath the surface of what was presented to *why* it is included in the case may reveal significant ideas for refutation during subsequent speeches.

Leading

Leading questions are the stereotype from courtroom drama, where the attorney sets up a series of questions which eventually lead the witness to break down and admit guilt, or something equally dramatic. The debater can likewise set up a series of questions, especially if some sort of logical relationship is the ultimate goal of the series. The examiner might try something along the lines of the following example.

Example: Leading Questions

EXAMINER: On contention II.B, what was your supporting evidence?

RESPONDENT: We cited a study calling for federal intervention.

EXAMINER: Was the study done by the federal government?

RESPONDENT: No, it was done by Zwigler Research.

EXAMINER: Did the federal government commission and pay Zwigler to do the study?

RESPONDENT: Well, yes, they did have a federal contract.

EXAMINER: What was the date?

RESPONDENT: October 1972.

EXAMINER: Was there a presidential election that year?

RESPONDENT: Yes, I believe so.

EXAMINER: Could money influence the results of a study?

RESPONDENT: I'm not sure what you're getting at.

EXAMINER: Suppose you were hired to mow somebody's lawn, would you do it the way they wanted?

RESPONDENT: I guess so.

EXAMINER: Is it possible such bias might creep into a study report as well.

RESPONDENT: I suppose it's possible.

EXAMINER: Was President Nixon running for reelection that year?

RESPONDENT: I don't know.

EXAMINER: Well, he was, and if we later introduce evidence showing he strongly favored federal intervention in this area as a theme in his campaign, are you still willing to stand by an argument whose only support is a twenty-year-old study, done at the request and support of the federal government, which exactly concludes what the incumbent wanted it to conclude and which was issued just in time for the November election?

RESPONDENT: Well, (pause) you'd have to show me where there's a problem.

EXAMINER: Would a reasonable person at least have cause to wonder?

RESPONDENT: Well, (pause) I'm not so sure. (pause) We thought it was pretty good.

EXAMINER: Thank you, let's now turn to contention III. Can you restate your title of this contention for me?

As you can see, the examiner set up a series of questions designed to reveal a weakness in the opposition's case. While the respondent never admitted this weakness, most people in the audience would be impressed by the damaged credibility of the evidence and by the team that proved it, and they would be ready for subsequent refutation (not during the cross-examination, but in a following speech) which would attempt to destroy the argument and the issue it supported on the basis that the evidence used was certainly outdated and probably biased. If this issue were a major one for the opponents, then it would be worth the time spent to reveal this weakness and set up later refutation. The sequence above would have to be a major objective of the examiner, for it takes about one and one-half minutes to complete. The time would be well-spent for a major idea, but not for a minor evidence challenge. Notice how the examiner used a combination of direct, open, and probe questions to set up a series. Effective cross-examination will not only have a series of single questions, but will also be able to build upon the answers.

The examiner can prepare in advance a variety of strategies based on the alternative responses which might come. For example, a well-prepared examiner will think: "What will I do if the opponent answers this way? What if the opponent says this or that? What follow-up questions can I predict no matter which way the response goes?" Such advance analysis will keep the examiner in charge of the focus and direction of the cross-examination.

The respondent can also prepare, in advance, possible answers. The best way is to work with your partner and ask each other the most difficult questions about your case, and practice giving responses which leave you on your own territory. As in refutation, the best preparation is a solid case which you have developed carefully, supported well, and know fully. In practice sessions with other team members, you can develop potential questions and listen to those developed by others. The use of video tape can be of tremendous benefit, enabling you to see yourself in both positions of asking and answering questions.

Remember, both examiner and respondent want to build their credibility by paying attention to the four factors mentioned above. They both want to clarify issues and ideas so that the basis for the debate will be focused. In addition, the examiner wants to probe the opponent's case and reasoning for weaknesses, while the respondent desires to defend issues, arguments, evidence, and reasoning.

Application of Cross-Examination

It is possible to apply skills learned in the cross-examination process to nondebate settings as well. You can transfer skills in answering questions to your classrooms where teachers often ask direct, open-ended, or probing questions about class related work. "Did you read last night's assignment? What did you think about it? Would you like to see this area as part of a final project?" are examples of the three types of questions as they might be used in the classroom. Likewise, if you are tactful about it, you can employ questioning strategies to gain information from your teachers. Such inquiries as: "What are the page numbers for tonight's reading? How do you rate the importance of this novel? Is this the type of item likely to appear on the final exam?" are ways you can (perhaps you already have) use questioning skills in the classroom. By being prepared with both questions and possible answers to potential questions, you can become a more effective student and leave a strong impression on your teachers.

In public involvement, you may find yourself participating in community activities. You can use skills in asking and answering questions in such settings as civic meetings, club activities, councils, boards, and commission hearings, or those involving volunteer organizations such as scouts or service groups. The ability to ask cogent questions and to respond spontaneously is a skill which marks a leader and someone who will have impact on the outcome of a meeting.

Careers almost always begin with interviews, and interviews are largely a question-and-answer exchange. Most interviews will employ a variety of direct, open, and probe questions, and so your practice in responding to them in the debate setting can prepare you to complete a successful interview.

Finally, many students involved in debate consider a career in law. Certainly the ability to phrase precise questions will be an asset to any attorney, whether in the courtroom or in client or interview situations. Even if one does not wind up with the dramatic courtroom confession of television fame, there are still multiple opportunities to talk to clients, negotiate contracts, and interview parties in disputes. An important aspect of the courtroom is an attorney's examination of prospective jurors. This process, called *voir dire*, provides an excellent opportunity for you to observe attorneys using cross-examination skills and techniques.

Cross-examination skills are valuable in the debate setting and have wide application to a variety of situations in school and other areas. All of these situations will be better if you are skilled in question-and-answer techniques.

Summary of the Principles of Cross-Examination

You can see from this introduction that cross-examination is a major item in debate, even though it has only a few minutes in the format. Remember that it is not a time to argue, but a time to discover ideas which you can later use for argument. Most judges will not remember what you specifically said or did during cross-examination unless you bring it up later. In fact, judges usually do not take notes during the cross-examination periods; therefore, if you want your cross-examination results to be effective, you must bring them up during subsequent refutation or defense.

One area which is noticed and remains in the mind of the audience is the impression you create during your presentation, especially during cross-examination. How you handle yourself while asking and answering questions will leave a lasting impression about your credibility. Remember to indicate to your listeners that you are dynamic, expert, trustworthy, and pleasant. Any other message runs the risk of downgrading your presentation and probably your score and your chances of winning the ballot.

In summation, three principles are important to remember:

1. The cross-examination period, though relatively short, can be critically important for setting up arguments which you will use later in the debate.

2. Most judges will not remember, nor apply, what you say in cross-examination unless you bring it up again in subsequent speeches.

3. The manner of questioning and answering affects your ethos. Communicate through your manner that you are dynamic, expert, trustworthy, and pleasant.

Until now, the principles which we have discussed have application to all the speakers in a debate. It is now time to focus on the specific goals and obligations of each speaker position. Those duties are the subject of chapter 8.

8

Speakers' Duties in Presenting the Debate

We mentioned earlier that wise speakers budget their speaking time with great care. There is good reason to be careful, namely that there is much to be done in a short amount of time. But when debaters actually come to the platform to address the audience, they must also realize that each of the eight speeches and four cross-examinations in a typical debate is made under somewhat different circumstances. Obviously, the first constructive speaker has the full attention of the audience, while the last rebuttal speaker faces an audience which is probably weary and may be somewhat confused by the claims and counterclaims of the previous eleven speaking or questioning periods. Each speaker, therefore, may have somewhat different duties to perform in order to convince the audience. The debate situation keeps changing, and the debater must adapt to those changes.

With the changeability of the debate situation in mind, we will now consider some of the factors each speaker should understand. Note that the debate should be viewed as a sequence of opposing ideas—what the first negative says, for example, may force the second affirmative to revise a previously planned speech in order to meet the attack on the affirmative case. Therefore, it is unwise for a team to insist on a rigid time budget for speeches after the first affirmative. It is even more injudicious, however, for one team to ignore what its opponents have said—forgetting that the audience has heard those other arguments as well as their own. A sure sign of a poor debate team is a second affirmative who acts as if the first negative had never spoken.

The following suggestions are, therefore, intended as a guide rather than absolute time limits. The duties are generally the same in most debates, although there may be some room for adaptation as well.

Constructive Speeches

First Affirmative Constructive

This speaker states the proposition for debate, defines any terms likely to prove troublesome, and launches the affirmative line of argument. It is advisable for this speaker to outline the entire affirmative case with great clarity, indicating which issues and arguments will be developed in the second affirmative.

The first affirmative constructive, in short, should get the debate started with a clear outline of the affirmative's philosophy in relation to the proposition with any related interpretations, limitations, or restrictions. Every word of the proposition need not be defined, only those which may be ambiguous or which the affirmative understands to have a technical or unusual meaning in the debate. A debate in which both sides quibble extensively about a definition is usually won by the negative since such quibbling distracts the affirmative from its job of proving the proposition.

If you are debating a value-oriented proposition, then this speech must outline a clear value system to be applied in the analysis. A debater dealing with a policy question must present a compelling need or problem area and often will also indicate the plan to solve that need.

Absolute clarity is the aim of the first speaker. Ordinarily, the audience can get a clear picture of the whole affirmative if the speaker outlines for them the issues and arguments to be discussed and identifies any reserved until the second affirmative. A clear summary at the end of this speech, which reviews the outline of the affirmative case as a whole, will add emphasis to the case and probably save confusion later on.

In chapter 2 we mentioned a possible time budget for this speech. The exact time apportionment may differ from speaker to speaker, but the important factor is that you plan each minute of the speech. As you begin your first affirmative constructive, take a few minutes to review those time suggestions. Remember that you need an introduction and definition of key terms of the proposition; a statement of the affirmative philosophy, including a value criterion if debating a value-oriented topic; an outline preview of the entire affirmative case, indicating which topics will be covered by your partner; presentation of the affirmative case including supporting arguments; and a final summary of the entire case. Ideally, even if you will not be the first affirmative speaker, but will take on the duties of the second affirmative, you should still be involved in the writing of the first speech. You will have to defend it in the second affirmative, so you must be completely familiar with its development and contents. Two team members working together can produce a document which both can then support.

First Negative Constructive

The duties in this speech are two: first, to state the negative's philosophy towards the proposition; and second, to indicate the manner in which the negative will attempt to refute the affirmative's case.

In some respects, the first negative constructive is the most important speech in the entire debate. We discussed earlier that the negative team must decide on its method of attack before the debate. The negative can merely refute whatever the affirmative says. It can attack the value system or offer an alternative. It can attack the need argument or the plan; offer its own substitute value system or solution, admitting a problem with the one in the status quo; or both. But once the first negative indicates which direction the team will take, then the negative must follow through. They cannot come back in a later speech with another approach without greatly weakening their position.

Thus, the first negative speaker indicates areas of clash. The affirmative speakers, after all, must create a belief in the truth of a proposition, using a number of subpropositions or issues at each step. Each of these assertions is like a link in a chain; if any one of them is broken, the chain ceases to exist. The negative usually chooses, therefore, to attack the weakest links in the chain of argument—to clash with those issues it feels best able to refute. A thoughtful affirmative speaker will listen carefully to the first negative speech to determine the course of the negative attack and thus prepare its defenses.

Some negative teams will try to devote this entire speech to pure refutation, hoping to reserve their constructive arguments for their second speech and thus outwit the affirmative by introducing constructive arguments, countervalues, or even counterplans late in the debate. Such strategy is of doubtful value since it essentially avoids the real issues of the debate. Moreover, a practical time disadvantage is that the second negative speaker then has to handle refutation and counterrefutation while trying to squeeze the entire constructive argument into half a speech.

The first negative speaker also has the last opportunity to accept or reject the definitions offered by the affirmative. Silence at this point is assent. Some speakers say explicitly that they accept the definitions, and we prefer this approach because it minimizes confusion, but it is assumed that they are accepted unless otherwise noted. The affirmative has a right, logically, to make sure that both its opponents and the audience understand clearly what the proposition means—hence the definition of troublesome terms. But the affirmative is obliged to support the entire proposition, as its minimum duty, and the negative should object to definitions which actually lessen the meaning of the proposition for debate. The key question in respect to definition, then, becomes, "Does the affirmative define the proposition in a reasonable manner, or does it attempt to change it in an unreasonable manner?" Unless a significant change is made in a definition, the negative should not quibble over it.

The first negative speech—and all speeches which follow—should acknowledge at the outset what the preceding speaker has said. If the first negative has no intention of spending time immediately on direct refutation of the first affirmative, it would be wise to preview for the audience the areas to be covered in the speech. In fact, a good initial preview is helpful in each speech. Without such an introduction, the audience may reach one of two conclusions: the speaker has failed to understand the opponents' arguments; or worse, that the speaker is unable to reply to them. In the same way, any important material discussed in cross-examination should be included with a reference to the fact that it comes from the cross-examination period.

Both negative speakers should make it clear to the audience that the burden of proof for the proposition lies with the affirmative. The negative ought to make an initial analysis of the proposition in order to do this. Without such explicit analysis, the affirmative may get by (and many affirmative speakers do) with supporting a much lighter burden of proof than is their responsibility.

As the debate increases in complexity, laying out precise time budgets for the speeches becomes increasingly difficult. Start with the suggestions presented earlier, and as you become proficient in talking about arguments and issues, you will begin to make adaptations which suit you and the particular debate. Almost always, you will need an introduction, discussion of definitions, acknowledgment of affirmative arguments (and refutation if desired), analysis of the proposition from the negative view—the negative philosophy, presentation of a negative case with supporting arguments, and a summary of both cases to this point in the debate.

Second Affirmative Constructive

The major issues of the debate have probably been stated by the time the second affirmative rises to speak. The primary duties of this speaker, therefore, will include reasserting the affirmative point of view and concluding the case for the team.

The negative speaker has no doubt raised some objections which the affirmative speaker must at least acknowledge. If desired, these objections can be addressed directly (and briefly) at the start of the speech. An alternative which we prefer is to mention them briefly in a preview, indicating that these objections will be discussed at the appropriate point in the affirmative case outline. We like this format better because it keeps the debate on affirmative ground and reminds the audience of the affirmative outline. Since this speech is essentially a constructive, the second affirmative must overcome the temptation to spend too much time on refutation while ignoring the support for the case. Any items discussed in cross-examination should be included here as well, mentioning that they were initiated during the cross-examination period. These may be items brought up by either team, but which require response at the appropriate place on the affirmative outline. It bears repeating here that a key to persuasion for the affirmative is to keep the affirmative constructive outline constantly in the minds of the listeners.

It has been quite common in policy topics for the second affirmative to offer the solution or plant, while the first affirmative concentrates on attacking the status quo or creating the need issue. Currently, more teams present the entire case in the first affirmative so that the audience can get the whole picture. Since this practice has resulted in presenting more areas in the first speech, each area is now given less time. Then in the second affirmative, the team can expand upon those areas needing additional support, perhaps presenting advantages as new constructive material. If the first affirmative, however, has failed to convince the audience that there is a real, significant problem, it is useless to present a plan to solve it. Therefore, the first step of any second affirmative is to make a brief restatement of the affirmative case as a whole, acknowledging the negative attacks, and in policy debates, resupporting the need issue if it seems necessary. The effective establishment of the need issue then leads to the development of a solution, whether that solution is presented in the first affirmative or is held until the second.

On the other hand, in a value-oriented topic, the second affirmative may deal with extension of the affirmative case and refutation of the negative attacks. Usually, the practice has been to present the entire case in the first affirmative and allow the second affirmative to defend the whole outline. One alternative which some teams use is for the second affirmative to present value benefits which they predict will follow from the adoption of the value they defend.

The alternatives given above are largely a matter of personal or team preference or strategy. Judges may get used to a certain practice in their area, and so if your strategy is at variance to this norm, be especially clear in your initial preview of the affirmative division of labor.

The speech should end with a double summary, with the speaker restating both cases as they have appeared up to that point. The second affirmative needs a longer summary than the first affirmative because of the negative attack which has intervened. A practical plan for this speech might be a restatement of the affirmative case so far; acknowledgment (with refutation) of the negative attack; application of solutions or benefits, either as outlined by your partner or as new material; double summary; and analysis of the debate to this point comparing the affirmative and negative cases.

Second Negative Constructive

The primary job of this speaker is to contrast the entire negative case against the entire affirmative case. This contrast is accomplished by analyzing the whole debate, centering the attack on the entire affirmative case, and evaluating it in terms of the negative view.

In many respects, the second negative has the freest hand in the debate, having heard the entire affirmative case. This speech can then be adapted to the specific affirmative in order to counter it. Material from three cross-examination periods is also available for inclusion in this speech. The second negative should outline the affirmative case, then the negative case, clarifying the clash of issues and directing attention to negative arguments which the affirmative has ignored or failed to answer adequately. Finally, after development of the negative case, this speaker should recapitulate the whole debate as clearly as possible in a double summary and comparison.

Many debates are won or lost by this speech. If the affirmative has presented a well-organized, clear set of arguments, this speech represents the last chance for the negative to advance constructive arguments against it. Remember that in the rebuttal period, the affirmative has two advantages it did not have in the constructive: (1) it no longer bears the great burden of introducing and establishing constructive arguments to support the burden of proof and can, for the first time, concentrate primarily on refutation; and (2) the affirmative has the final rebuttal. During the rebuttal, therefore, the affirmative is on more than even terms with the negative. Hence, it is imperative that the second negative establish a definite superiority for its side. Moreover, since the first rebuttal speaker is negative, some of the effect of that speech may be lost when an audience thinks of it as a mere extension of the second negative constructive.

A practical plan for the second negative constructive is one which allows efficient comparison of the two teams' cases. This speaker could begin with an outline of the affirmative case and refutation of main issues on the basis of the burden of proof and then provide a restatement of the negative case showing conflict with the affirmative. Taken together, these first steps constitute an analysis of the whole debate. The second negative can then apply the negative view to the whole affirmative case and provide a summary of both the affirmative and the negative, indicating conflict and the impact of the negative attack. This speaker must be especially careful to cover any new lines of argument which result from hearing the second affirmative. The first negative rebuttal can always continue previously issued attacks, but the second negative constructive is the last time to offer any new arguments.

Rebuttal Speeches

Clarifying Is Essential

Each rebuttal speech follows the same organizational plan, whether affirmative or negative. The rebuttal speakers must criticize the opposing case and defend their own.

The rebuttal period can be extremely confusing to an audience, even a trained judge, as well as to the debaters themselves. Very often, the most successful rebuttalist is the speaker who is merely very clear—the one who is able to clarify issues for the audience and who shows at each point precisely how the arguments compare to those of the opposition. In a rebuttal speech an accurate summary is often a decisive factor. Successful rebuttal requires a calm, crystalized overview of the whole case.

Discarding Minor Points

The prime virtue of the rebuttal speaker is an ability to reject, to discard, and to ignore the nonessentials. If you understand the main issues—and this depends largely on your preparation for the whole debate—you will know what is worth the expenditure of your time during the brief final speeches. Nothing is more futile than two debate teams, after forty or fifty minutes of speeches, quarreling about a minor point, such as the date of a quotation or the exact numbers in a statistical statement.

Thinking and Speaking in Outline Terms

It is essential that the rebuttal speaker think and speak in outline terms, thus making every issue clear. You have only two methods of approach: you can attack (or defend) either (1) arguments, or (2) evidence. Because time does not permit you to discuss every statement made by your opponents, you must make a series of rapid decisions. If you and your partner have been making double summaries throughout the debate, most of those decisions will already have been made. Preparation for the rebuttal speeches has to begin, in effect, with your first mental summary of the opposition. It is at this point of the rebuttal that careful listening proves its worth. The rebuttalist owes it to the audience to speak in outline terms, thus constantly contrasting and comparing the major points to show where the clash occurs. In this manner, you can help the audience make up its mind to reject the nonessentials and concentrate on the major issues.

Confusion in the rebuttal hurts the affirmative more than it does the negative, since it clouds the issues and hampers the affirmative's attempt to create a clear belief in their proposition. But confusion may hurt the negative as well if the audience is unable to make sense out of what the negative is trying to do. A confused audience may then remember only a well-organized affirmative case.

Emphasizing the Clash Between Cases

Emphasis in rebuttals should be on the clearly defined clash between the two cases. The audience is entitled to an honest comparison of the opposing sides. Any method which provides this comparison is useful, and any process which prevents it should be avoided. Hence, each rebuttal speaker has the same purpose.

Splitting the Rebuttal Duties

Since it is still a debate between teams of speakers, partners should cooperate in their rebuttal speeches. Usually, it is not advisable for each speaker to try to handle the details of the entire opposing case alone; lack of time will lead to superficial coverage. Instead, partners may split the rebuttal job between them, just as they split their constructive case between them. Duties of the first and second rebuttal speakers for each side differ only in minor details.

First Rebuttal (either side):
1. Outline of opponents' case contrasted to own case, with statement of points to be handled by partner
2. Refutation of at least one-half of the outline
3. Summary and outline of patrner's duties

Second Rebuttal (either side):
1. Summary of entire debate contrasting both cases
2. Refutation of remainder of outline

3. Final summary of entire debate, pointing out the clash between the two cases

Listening to Opposing Speakers

One of the debater's primary duties is to adapt the case to the changing situation as the clash continues. Unless you are able to make an accurate judgment about the opposing arguments, you will be unable to adapt; it thus becomes necessary for you to devise a careful, systematic approach to the problem of listening. Such an approach will not be difficult if you keep in mind the basic principle—that a debate is essentially a clash of opposing outlines.

A person listening intently to an ordinary speaker could easily make a single running outline, but in the debate situation much more is necessary. The listener needs to know what the assertions are, what their supports are, what their relationship is to the opposing case, and what possible replies might be made to key arguments. In other words, a full case analysis must go on while the opposing speaker is actually delivering a speech. Again, because time is limited, the method used must be both simple and efficient. In addition, it must be a system which can be used, without the need of recopying, to provide speaking notes for later speeches in the debate.

The best system is to use a *flow chart*, which will present a visual comparison between assertions and the methods of proof used by the speaker. Any method which provides space for a good outline of the opposing arguments will be useful; but it is best to include a statement of proofs as well, so that the entire opposing case can be seen at a glance. If this procedure is followed throughout the debate, rebuttal speeches can be prepared directly from the analysis chart without recopying any material.

In order to keep track of the flow of the debate, some debaters use a simple two column sheet made by drawing a single line down the middle of a blank page. Others prefer a four column chart based on the same principle, but which allows the listing of all four speakers horizontally (see fig. 8.1).

This four-column flow-chart is fairly useful, but unless very

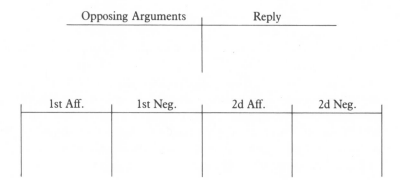

Fig. 8.1. Debate flow-chart samples.

large sheets of paper are used, it leaves little room on the sheet for noting types of proof. The disadvantages of using the four-column system are that you may need to write in such small hand-writing that it is not useful for speaking notes in later speeches, and large sheets are cumbersome when used for speaking notes. The main advantage of this system is that it shows all four speech outlines at a glance, matched horizontally.

The Case Analysis Chart (table 8.1) is another means of solving the problem of intelligently analyzing the case of opposing speakers. It would be wise for a team to prepare such a chart of its own case in advance in order to provide instant cross-reference during the debate. The advantages of this type of chart are several: it focuses attention on the basic elements of assertion and proof, it provides quick reference to logical connections between parts of the opposing case, and it can be carried to the platform for speaking notes without any further changes. If you also have a similar outline of your own case, you are prepared to deliver an accurate double summary of both cases during each speech in the debate. Try these methods out and find which one or which combination works best for you as you advance in your debating skills.

Summary of Speakers' Duties

This chapter was designed to present some guidelines about the duties each speaker will have in a debate. Although there is some slight variation between the specific duties found in value questions and policy questions, the basics are pretty much the same. One of the challenges of becoming a successful debater is to learn about the duties of each position. You will be a stronger debater, and a better partner, if you try debating in each position, and we urge you to do so often.

Five Principles to Remember

There are five principles which each speaker needs to remember:
1. Each speech in a debate has a different objective.
2. Each part of each speech has a definite duty to fulfill.
3. Budgeting of time is absolutely necessary to make sure that these duties are fulfilled.
4. Adaptation to the changing circumstances during the debate requires careful listening to opposing speakers.
5. All speakers must be as clear as possible about their own argument, about their reactions to those of their opponents, and about the relation of both to the debate as a whole.

Next, we will try to bring together the final skill area needed in good debating—your ability to use effective language and delivery so that your ideas will have both clarity and impact.

Table 8.1
The Case Analysis Chart

	Assertions	Methods of Proof	Comments
FIRST SPEAKER	*Constructive* List here, in outline form, the major assertions of the opposing speaker.	List here, opposite each item in the left column, the proof advanced to support each assertion. Make a note of its type—for example, quotation, statistics, reasoning alone, or no proof given.	List here either: 1. General comments opposite any item. *or* 2. Arguments you plan to use in refutation of each item. *Important Note:* It is most essential to fill out the first two columns as you listen to your opponent. This third column may be developed during your partner's speech, or it may even be left blank since you will have to extemporize your reply in any case. The important point one must remember is to avoid wasting time on thinking up replies at the cost of missing a part of the opposing speech.
	Rebuttal		

Repeat the process for all four opposing speeches.

Constructive			
Rebuttal			
SECOND SPEAKER			

9

Language and Delivery in Presenting the Debate

The essential idea to remember about debate style and debate delivery is a simple one: Debate, as the art of formal oral controversy, is a type of public speaking. Although *The Debater's Guide* cannot pretend to replace a course in public speaking, it is useful to call attention to some fundamental principles which are common to debate and to other types of public speaking as well.

The Use of Verbal and Nonverbal Factors

As a type of public speaking, debate is an oral means of presenting ideas to an audience in an organized manner. Two thousand years ago, the Roman orator Cicero laid down three duties for a speaker which are just as relevant for today's debater: (1) to be clear, so the audience can understand what is said; (2) to be interesting, so the audience will want to listen; and (3) to be persuasive or convincing, so the audience will agree.

In striving to accomplish these goals, language and actual physical delivery—use of voice and body to communicate verbally and nonverbally—are the chief factors to consider after the speeches are organized. And both are the means by which the debate speech is actually brought to the audience.

The Audience

Effective style (language) and delivery are impossible without careful consideration of the audience. Who are the listeners and watchers? What are their ages, their professions, their backgrounds? What are their prejudices, their predispositions? A set of phrases useful for a student audience might not create a favorable impression among an audience of bank managers. And the loud, gesture-punctuated speech which serves for an audience of a thousand people might seem awkward when delivered in a small room to only a few people.

There are two main considerations relating to the audience—its character and its size. In general, the character of the audience affects the language to be used for maximum effectiveness. That is, since any speaker must use language which is intelligible to the listeners, any adaptation to be made because of the age, education, or profession of the audience will be made in terms of the language employed. Delivery methods are not likely to be altered for such reasons. A high school audience, for example, might not understand the term *reciprocal trade agreement* without some explanation, while a group of adult merchants would probably need no explanation. When in doubt about such terms, use both the technical term and a synonym or a brief explanation the first time it is used in the debate. After the term has been explained once or twice, it can probably be used safely without further concern.

The size of the audience makes some difference in the type of delivery the speaker should use. If there are a thousand people in an auditorium, gestures must be made larger, facial expressions will have to be more pronounced, and words must be delivered more slowly. Otherwise, some of the audience will not be able to hear or see the speaker. Before a smaller group, especially in a small room, delivery should be more restrained, because the audience can hear and see each slight change in facial expression or tone of voice. Debaters should especially avoid being overly loud in small rooms. Although this advice is difficult to remember as the issues become more intense and the debate more active, try to remember it.

The Judge as Audience

A vast majority of school debates are delivered before one judge, often a teacher, although there may be as many as three or five judges if the debate is one of the finals in a tournament. Occasionally, a debate may be delivered to a fairly large group of people, one of whom is to cast the ballot to decide the debate. Debaters should understand the true function of the judge in order to plan their speeches effectively. The *judge* appears in the debate situation as a critical observer of your attempt to persuade an audience to accept or reject the proposition. This principle is extremely important because it determines not only the judge's position but also the speakers' duties. What it means is that every effective debater must also be an effective public speaker.

Some debaters have the mistaken idea that the judge in a debate is like the judge in a courtroom without a jury, where lawyers stand up to deliver oral briefs. Therefore, they think the ideal debater is one who merely delivers as many facts as possible in as short a time as possible and leaves it up to the judge to sort out all the pieces. Or they feel free to use highly specialized terms, as if all parties knew exactly what the words meant. Finally, these debaters feel that delivery is unimportant, and they merely read long quotations in a dull monotone while looking down at their cards or paper and ignoring the people in the room. Such speakers will profit little from their debate experience, for they will find no real audience in later life that fits this false concept of the debate speaking situation. Indeed, most real audiences would not tolerate that style with as much patience as many debate judges try to exhibit.

It would be better to think of the debater as a person speaking to a jury, under the watchful eye of a judge. In this case, both judge and jury require consideration. For this reason, the debater will address the debate judge as part of a larger audience.

It is the judge's task to evaluate the job you do in persuading that larger audience.

The Language of Debate

Although it is impossible to encompass the complex subject of language in a few pages, there are three major ideas which the debater should keep in mind:

1. The language of debate must be intelligible to the audience.
2. It should be free of jargon and clichés.
3. It should, through the skillful use of transitions, help the audience to understand the progress of the debate.

Make the Language Intelligible.   Most debate topics deal with complex issues such as economics, value systems, politics, international affairs, or combinations of these. Therefore, the debate speaker enters into highly specialized fields of knowledge which may be unfamiliar to the audience. The first responsibility is to define the unfamiliar words being used—for instance, many audiences would be unfamiliar with the distinction between *preventative war* and *pre-emptive war*. It is also the debaters' responsibility to clarify terms to which they want to attach special meanings for purposes of the debate. For example, many policy debates have plans which involve a *commission* or *board* to administer the policy proposed in the topic. In a value-oriented topic, the affirmative may need to define a hierarchy of *more important* values. In either case, the audience is entitled to know what such terms mean to the speaker who uses them. A useful method in this respect is to link the word with a synonym the first few times it is used. In defining terms in the proposition itself, many affirmative speakers find it effective to repeat the whole proposition after the definition, substituting their definitions for the defined words. For example, "Resolved: That the State Department of the United States should offer to exchange ambassadors and other diplomatic representatives with the government of Cuba. (Resolved: That the United States should recognize Cuba.)"

Once a term is used with a special meaning, it must be used consistently in that meaning throughout the debate.

How many terms need definitions? The answer, always a matter of judgment, is based on the character of the audience and its probable familiarity with the subject. Two kinds of terms nearly always need definition, at least by synonym: first, terms which may be ambiguous because there are two, or more, possible meanings available (*tariff policy* or *environmental protection*); and second, terms with an ordinary meaning which the speaker wishes to use in an unusual way (*recognize* when the speaker means exchange only one ambassador and prohibit other relations, or *constitutional rights* to mean all rights contained in or inferred from the Constitution).

As a practical matter, in debates addressed to judges within a larger audience, the debater can simply define key terms at their first use and refer to synonyms for one or two times after that. Regardless of the audience, the speaker can never assume that any single statement will be remembered during the entire debate. Audiences may be inattentive or forgetful or may not understand completely the first time. Hence, you can see the value of repetition of important words and ideas.

Avoid Jargon and Clichés.   Debaters sometimes live in a semantic world of their own, using over and over again the same stereotyped expressions. There is nothing wrong with using a technical term like, *burden of proof* or *fallacy*, if the audience is told what it means, since such terms can serve a practical purpose during the course of a debate. On the other hand, your originality will eventually suffer if you rely on a series of commonplace terms without using more pertinent language. Because adaptability is a key to debate success, anything which restricts the freedom of language is a handicap.

In chapter 6, we listed some common clichés in refutation which also occur throughout the debate. A little attention to the actual speaking habits of debaters will no doubt reveal many more of these expressions. For instance, some of the following examples might be noted.

Avoid:	*Because:*	*Use instead:*
"my worthy opponents" or "the opposition"	May sound sarcastic; archaic, at best; encourages antagonism	"the affirmative speakers"
"honorable judges" (in introduction)	Archaic, may sound sarcastic.	"Gentlemen," or "ladies and gentlemen"
"I would like to run down the arguments of the opposition"	Ambiguous.	"I would like to review the arguments of the affirmative"
"My partner has proved conclusively that"	Argumentative without further proof.	"My partner has outlined the reasons for"

Use Transitions.   Any debate can confuse an audience. Conversely, any debater who can clarify matters for the audience will stand a better chance of getting ideas accepted. Transitions help the audience follow the progress of the debate.

One of the major faults in school debating is a failure to make clear to the audience the exact nature of the outline upon which the team's case is built. Two speakers will sometimes spend fifteen to twenty minutes reciting statistics, quotations, and facts, but will completely fail to show how all these things fit together. It is quite possible for a team to think in outline terms throughout the debate, assuming that the audience will somehow follow their line of reasoning; yet this same team may neglect to help the audience by not using the verbal signposts which can do so much for clarity.

Why are verbal signposts so necessary in oral discourse? Their value is readily understood if one can imagine looking at a page of written language that has no capital letters, no punctuation, no paragraph indentations, and no bold-face headings to indicate its parts and sections. The nature of oral discourse is even less clear as it strikes the ears of the audience, since they cannot stop, pause, and go back two or three lines to try to pick out the main ideas. The only "punctuation" in a speech comes from the speaker. Consequently, and you have heard us say this before, it is imperative to think and to speak in outline terms.

This advice does not mean that it is necessary to say, "Now I will turn to part III. A. of my case." It does mean, however, that the speaker must skillfully use the ordinary transitional devices which keep the audience informed of the outline or organization at every step. As a general rule, a debater should never end one part of the case outline without telling the audience explicitly that one part has ended and another part is about to begin.

Any standard textbook of grammar or public speaking can supply a large list of transitional devices, but the debater should pay particular attention to the three basic types.

1. Transitions of Introduction:
   next
   another
   a further
   a second
   a third
   now let us turn to
   What does this mean?
2. Transitions of Summary:
   in conclusion
   in summary
   finally
   we have now seen that
   these three facts (repeat them briefly)
   before going to speak about (next item)
3. Transitions of Logical Conclusion
   therefore
   consequently
   hence
   we can now conclude that
   thus
   these facts demonstrate that

Any reminder or cross reference is helpful to an audience. It serves as useful repetition which may help to prove the argument.

Characteristics of Good Delivery

Delivery is the term we use to describe the communication of your ideas to an audience with words, gestures, facial expressions, and any other external means at your disposal (including visual aids). Mere recitation of words does not constitute good delivery. Therefore, you should examine carefully the following characteristics of good delivery.

Posture. Posture should be natural to you and yet remain dignified.

1. Do not lean on desks, chairs, or the lectern.
2. Do not sway from side to side.
3. Do not stand stiffly in one position.
4. Occasional movement is helpful to provide variety and to release some of your natural tensions and energy.
5. Avoid positions which make you feel strained or tensely unnatural or which will appear awkward.

Position of Arms and Hands. Arms and hands should be held naturally, but should never be fixed in one position.

1. Varying the position of arms and hands from time to time will provide variety for the audience and will further release your tensions.
2. Do not lock arms behind your back or in front of you.
3. Do not do the same thing all the time. Change positions often.
4. Never attempt a gesture unless it feels natural to you.
5. Avoid toying with objects (such as pens, pencils, or note cards) and clasping or wringing your hands, since these actions will distract your audience from what you have to say.

Eye Contact. You should establish eye contact with the people in your audience.

1. Watch the facial expressions of the individuals in the audience to see how they are receiving what you say.
2. Make sure that you include every person in your audience, while paying special attention to your judge.

3. Try to speak to individual persons instead of to the audience as a mass.

4. Avoid looking out windows, over heads, and down.

Attitude.   Your attitude (as the audience sees it) should be one of confidence in the value and importance of what you are saying.

1. Enthusiasm concerning the subject often carries over to an audience.

2. Confidence in what you are to say will frequently give you confidence in your ability to deliver the material as well.

3. Avoid an appearance of arrogance or of being apologetic.

Voice.   Variety in the use of your voice is the key to being clear and interesting.

1. Slow down and stress key words when you wish to emphasize an idea.

2. Speed up slightly when telling a story or listing factual details which illustrate a main point.

3. Pause slightly between major ideas for emphasis.

4. Vary your volume and your pitch to suit the material and the size of the room.

5. Avoid monotones.

Above all, strive for variety. If there is one principle to be applied for effective delivery of a speech, it is probably this: Be varied—never do the same thing all the time.

Special Problems in Debate Delivery

Some problems occur in debating that are not faced by the ordinary public speaker; other problems, like the use of notes, occur in other types of speaking, but not in the same way. We would like to note briefly the areas posing special problems for the debate speaker including: attitude of speakers, extempore ideal, memory and use of notes, speed of delivery, reading aloud, and visual aids.

Attitude of Speakers

Debate is controversial and controversy often becomes heated. However, nothing is gained by attempting to discredit your opponents. The debate speaker should show respect for opponents and for the worth of ideas. Debaters should display courtesy and fair-mindedness at all times. Certainly, it is not realistic to take a right-or-wrong attitude toward the debate—to act as if you and your partner have all the correct answers, while the opposing team has nothing but ignorance and stupidity on its side.

Many close debates may be won or lost by attitude. Arrogance is the loser. Speakers should never forget that a good debate is an honest attempt to provide the audience with two different answers to the question posed in the proposition. The audience is entitled to make up its mind on the basis of a rational discussion of the issues, not on emotionalism.

Extempore Ideal

Adaptation is the key to successful debating. Every speaker who comes after the first affirmative constructive has to make some adjustment, and it is only the good extemporaneous speaker who can do so intelligently. The ideal is to know your own case so well, in outline form, that you can easily recall it as you speak and thus adapt the wording of it to the situation at hand.

Memory and Use of Notes

Extempore speaking from notes requires clear understanding, rather than a prodigious memory. That is, wise use of notes can leave the speaker free to use personal phrasing for ideas, free to maintain eye contact with the audience, and free to use vocal variety of pitch, volume, and rate as appropriate. The only basic requirement is that the speaker must understand clearly the purpose of notes. Notes are not simply small manuscripts to be read aloud.

The speaker who wishes to extemporize a speech—that is, to deliver a speech in a somewhat spontaneous manner based on careful, previous preparation of a body of material—will carry to the speaking platform two kinds of written materials: first, an outline of the speech; and second, items to be read aloud or referred to during the speech. In a debate, you should have your own case outline memorized so well that you will probably need to think only about the second type of materials. You should first decide on a standard size and shape for your notes—usually a four-by-six-inch note card is preferred because cards are interchangeable and can be easily rearranged to fit opposing arguments. Avoid flimsy sheets which tear easily or which rattle audibly when held in the hand. Write notes large enough to be seen easily while speaking. If notes are too small, the card will have to be held in front of the eyes, thus distracting the audience and hampering eye contact.

If a speaker remembers to strive constantly to speak in outline form, then note cards will fall readily into definite patterns. Some cards will contain assertions, others will contain supports for those assertions, and still others will give details of support. If the case is well outlined, it should be possible to lay out every card in a note file in its exact position on the outline. A note card that is difficult to classify can mean that the note refers to two separate issues (in which case, an extra copy is useful), or that the speaker does not yet fully understand the case, or that the note card belongs in another section of the file for use against possible opponents or in building another case.

Speed of Delivery

Some debaters, especially those who are still somewhat inexperienced, seem to think that the ideal speech is one delivered at a machine-gun rate. Most Americans speak at an average rate of 120 to 150 words per minute. Thus, the debater who races on for ten minutes at 250 words per minute is going to attract attention—it will most likely be unfavorable. A good delivery maxim is that the speaker should avoid any mannerism which calls attention to itself and away from the ideas. Consequently, it is wise to avoid seeming hasty and frantic by trying to cram a twenty-minute speech in the allotted time. It is of great importance to remember this guideline in the rebuttal speeches, where confusion is already probable because of the complex debate clash. A hurried delivery is often a sign of poor case analysis because the debater is uncertain and tries to throw in every conceivable idea and fact in hope that one of them will work. Obviously, this speaker is unable to make rational judgments about which ideas and arguments are valuable. The intelligent debater selects only the best ideas and arguments before rising to speak and does not try to deluge the audience with a flood of words.

Reading Aloud

Reading aloud is more difficult than it seems because of the dangers to effective communication with the audience. Three principles of good delivery must be emphasized in reading:

1. The principle of emphasis: making the meaning of the text clear by stressing key words and avoiding monotones.
2. The principle of audience contact: keeping eye contact with the audience by constant glances and by avoiding fastening your eyes only on the paper.
3. The principle of variety of speed: varying the rate and the length of pauses and avoiding the tendency to accelerate. Most speakers tend to speed up while reading.

Visual Aids

Some debaters like to use visual aids—charts, diagrams, or objects—to clarify complex ideas during a debate. While their use is infrequent, graphs and diagrams can be useful for outlining complicated financial relationships, such as budget allotments for various parts of a program or changes over time. If visual aids are used, however, they must be made available to both sides in the debate. They should be removed from sight after use, but must be kept available if the other side wishes to discuss them during later speeches.

Visual aids have several inherent drawbacks, and therefore should be carefully executed and well used. The user should keep in mind that clarity is the chief goal desired. The following hints for the use of visual aids may be helpful:

1. Make the aid large enough to be seen clearly throughout the room.
2. In drawing, take care to produce heavy, dense lines which contrast strongly with the surface upon which they are drawn.
3. Eliminate excess detail.
4. Label the important parts using heavy letters.
5. Consider differentiating functions or structures by the use of contrasting colors.
6. Check your use of aids in practice before you attempt to use them in actual debates.

Summary of Rules for Delivery

Above all, then, the debater must remember to be a public speaker striving to secure acceptance of ideas by an audience. As such, you must analyze the audience, adapting your language and delivery to the circumstances of the situation. The debate situation, as you have seen, presents some special problems which every debater ought to keep in mind. For instance, the great amount of data usually presented in a debate makes it necessary that the debater be absolutely clear, keeping the audience informed at all times of exactly what is going on.

10

Virtues of the Ideal Debate Speaker

The Seven Talents Needed in Debating

Good debaters are speakers who can secure public acceptance of the ideas they propose, even though they are confronted by the organized opposition of others. Success under these difficult circumstances calls for a high degree of debate efficiency. As a final reminder, then, of the skills needed by the ideal debater, we offer you these seven talents to cultivate:

1. Ability to collect and to organize ideas.
2. Ability to subordinate ideas.
3. Ability to evaluate evidence.
4. Ability to see logical connections.
5. Ability to think and speak in outline terms.
6. Ability to speak convincingly, with clarity and impact.
7. Ability to adapt to new ideas.

Develop these abilities, cultivate them, and use them. Your debating and your future activities will improve as a result.

Appendix

Glossary

Selected Bibliography

Appendix:
The Stock Cases

Certain types of debate cases are easy to prepare and defend because they follow naturally from any logical analysis of a problem. You should become familiar with these stock cases for two reasons: first, they will probably be the backbone of your own arguments; and second, you must be prepared to refute the arguments of your opponents when they are based on the same lines of reasoning. The stock cases concerning propositions of policy are based on one or more of the following types of argument.

Affirmative

1. There is a need for a change from the status quo because certain evils exist which must be removed.

2. The affirmative proposal is the change needed because it will remove these evils.

3. The affirmative plan will also give certain advantages in addition to removing these evils.

4. The proposed plan has no real disadvantages.

5. The plan is practical.

6. Other proposed plans or repairs of the status quo either do not solve the problem or create new disadvantages. [Because this point may involve a lengthy process, it is usually held in reserve for refutation in the event that the negative offers a counterplan or a series of minor repairs to the status quo.]

The standard affirmative case often involves the first three items mentioned above—a need, a plan to solve that need, and some advantages—although it is enough to simply have a need plan. Another option found in debate tournaments is the comparative advantage approach discussed in chapter 5. That type of affirmative has steps 2 and 3 as its core and then may add any of those steps coming after. Our advice is to build as strong a case as research, time, and your communication skills will allow. Certainly, a well-prepared affirmative team will have considered all six items in developing a case.

Negative

The negative has a problem to solve before any approach can be made for an attack on the affirmative. The negative must choose one of the following plans of attack when dealing with a policy proposition, and it must stay with that plan throughout the debate.

1. The status quo is satisfactory. [This approach involves defending the present order or structure of things and, hence, forces the negative to show how good it is.]

2. The present system can be improved in minor ways to eliminate the problems. [This approach involves admitting that problems exist, but proposes that minor alterations, rather than major restructuring, are sufficient.]

3. There is another plan (other than the affirmative's proposal) which will solve the problem and is superior to the one offered by the affirmative. [This tactic is the counterplan and involves agreeing with the affirmative that there is a need for a change and that a major restructuring is required to solve that need.]

4. The affirmative proposal is inherently flawed. [This option may be combined easily with any of the other three for it is pure refutation. It involves spending all of the negative time in sheer attack on the affirmative contentions. Hence, the burden of proof rests squarely on the affirmative throughout the entire

debate. In the other options, some initial burden of proof begins to shift to the negative as well, especially in step 3.]

Some negative teams attempt to argue on all four levels by adopting an "even if" approach as a transition between each type. For example, they may begin by saying that the status quo is doing just fine, then say, "But even if you think there might be some problems, we could suggest some minor repairs to take care of them." After that they might try, "Even if you don't think these repairs will solve the alleged problems, there is a plan we could offer which is superior to the one presented by the affirmative." The offering of conditional counterplans is tried by some teams, but many judges frown on this combination approach because it is difficult to focus on a consistent negative position. A negative team combining any of these approaches assumes a complex burden that is difficult to communicate clearly to an audience. For the beginning debater, our advice is to use option number 4 as a primary approach and combine it with numbers 1 or 2.

The stock issues dealing with a value-oriented proposition can also form the basis for a case construction.

Affirmative

1. Identification of the value. [This step will be accomplished by defining key terms, setting a criterion by which the value and the debate may be evaluated, and determining any hierarchy which might be necessary.]

2. Application of the value. [The value should be related to the status quo in order to provide a context and perhaps determine presumption. The value should then be explicated to indicate how it links to the decision about the proposition, and finally, any beneficial results which follow logically from adopting the proposition may be outlined.]

Most affirmative cases develop along the lines of this two-part division. Thus, they have subcontentions under each part which develop the subissues listed.

Negative

1. Alternative value. [The negative may identify an alternative value which they contend to be competitive with and superior to the one offered by the affirmative. Sometimes the proposition will provide this option in its wording. For example, "Energy is more important than environment" clearly tells affirmative debaters to support the value of energy development, while the negative is directed to support the value of environmental protection.]

2. Alternative criterion. [The negative may wish to offer a different decision rule for evaluating the hierarchy of values or the debate.]

3. Value objections. [The negative may analyze the logical impacts of adopting the resolution and offer these objections as independent reasons for rejecting the proposition and the value it supports. These are not the same as offering direct refutation to the specifics of the affirmative case, but rather stem from the resolution itself. Many negative teams prepare these in advance of the debate.]

4. Straight refutation. [As in policy-oriented debate, the negative always has the option to attack the affirmative case point by point.]

Each of these options may be used in combination with the others to some degree. Our advice here is similar to that we gave to negative teams working in the area of policy propositions. Number 4 is always appropriate and can be easily combined with any others. As you advance in experience and confidence, you may attempt other combinations that are appropriate to your level of proficiency and the approach called for by the topic or the affirmative case.

The options presented above are intended to serve as an introduction to debate cases which are standard, or stock, approaches. While they have developed because they are useful in a wide variety of situations, they are not the only case formats. We suggest that you learn these fundamental approaches very thoroughly before you attempt more difficult types. Beginning debaters should remember that there are no strategic advantages to be gained from trying to run an unusual case against other beginners. It takes greater skill to present an unusual format and if the affirmative is not presented with clarity and precision, the affirmative will lose, not the surprised negative. Consult your instructors or the Selected Bibliography for suggested readings on advanced debate.

Glossary

AFFIRMATIVE SIDE. The speaker or team that undertakes to secure audience acceptance of the truth of the debate proposition.

ANALOGY. A type of argument which asserts that if the facts relating to A and the facts relating to B are alike in certain known respects, they will be alike in another respect.

ANALYSIS The process of thinking through a subject and discovering the issues; systematic inquiry.

ARGUMENT. An assertion which implies the result of reasoning or proof.

ASSERTION. An unsupported statement.

BRIEF. A carefully prepared, complete outline of one side in a debate, including the evidence to support each point.

BURDEN OF COMMUNICATION. The obligation of each debater to speak at a tone and rate which enables an audience to follow and to respond.

BURDEN OF PROOF. The obligation of debaters to support each of their assertions with some sort of proof.

BURDEN OF REBUTTAL. The obligation of debaters to advance the debate by responding to the arguments of the opponents. Sometimes called burden of rejoinder.

CASE. All the assembled proof available for determining the truth of the proposition (for the affirmative) or the untruth of the proposition (for the negative). The brief developed in full with analysis, reasoning, and evidence.

CAUSE. A type of argument which asserts that if fact A occurs, fact B will necessarily follow from it.

CEDA. See Cross Examination Debate Association.

CLAIM. The third part of Toulmin's system for argument analysis which is the conclusion.

CLASH. The direct opposition between the affirmative and the negative cases which is created by narrowing the controversy to its essential issues.

CONSTRUCTIVE SPEECH. The main speech in a debate for each speaker in which all issues to be considered in the debate are presented.

CONTENTION. An argumentative statement which forms a main heading in the constructive outline and which is in turn supported by arguments and evidence.

COUNTERPROPOSAL. In policy debates, it is a negative strategy which accepts the need issue, but offers an alternative solution.

COUNTERWARRANT. In value-oriented debate, it is a negative strategy which argues for the acceptance of an alternative value structure from that called for by the resolution.

CRITICISM. Comments provided by a judge or instructor with the intent of explaining an evaluation and indicating areas in need of improvement.

CROSS EXAMINATION. The process of asking questions of opposing speakers in debate.

CROSS EXAMINATION DEBATE ASSOCIATION (CEDA). A national organization with the purpose of promoting educational debate and dedicated to teaching the principles of persuasive and communicative argumentation. CEDA selects debate propositions, usually value-oriented, for debate at approved tournaments and compiles rankings of schools on the basis of performance at those tournaments.

DATA. The first part of the Toulmin system for analyzing argument which consists of bits of information or evidence such as statistics, quotations, or statements.

DEBATE. Formal oral controversy consisting of the systematic presentation of opposing arguments on a selected topic.

DELIVERY. The communication of ideas to an audience through verbal and nonverbal means.

DIRECT QUESTIONS. Very specific and focused cross-examination questions.

ETHOS. Aristotle's term for the perceived character of the speaker, credibility.

EVIDENCE. Matters of fact or opinion offered as support or proof for assertions advanced in the debate.

EXAMPLE. A type of argument which asserts a generalization based on the qualities of a specific instance or instances.

FALLACY. Any defect in reasoning which destroys its validity.

FLOW CHART. A tool used for taking notes during a debate which enables the debater or listener to keep track of the development of an argument throughout successive speeches. It represents the flow of argument in the debate.

FORENSICS. Speaking for judgment, often used to designate competitive interscholastic speech activities, such as debate. In this context, forensics is an educational activity primarily concerned with using an argumentative perspective in examining problems and communicating with people.

HIERARCHY. A system used to establish superior and inferior relationships between items. In value-oriented debate, a hierarchy indicates which value is held in higher regard than another.

ISSUE. A conclusion which must be proved in order to establish that the proposition should be adopted; it appears in the debate as a key assertion.

JUDGE. The person who evaluates a debate.

LEADING QUESTIONS. Cross-examination questions which establish a sequence or pattern, eventually building a logical conclusion.

LINCOLN-DOUGLAS DEBATE. One person versus one person debate format in the tradition of the historical debates between Abraham Lincoln and Stephen Douglas.

NATIONAL DEBATE TOURNAMENT (NDT). A term used as a shorthand reference to designate policy proposition debate and the style of presentation associated with it.

NDT. See National Debate Tournament.

NEED ISSUE. In policy-centered debate, it is an assertion by the affirmative side that there is need for a substantial change in the status quo.

NEGATIVE SIDE. The speaker or team which undertakes to prevent the affirmative side from securing acceptance of the debate proposition.

OBSERVATION. A preliminary remark which usually lays out a basic assumption or context before the presentation of contentions in a debate case.

OPEN QUESTIONS. Cross-examination questions which are very general in nature, allowing the respondent to give general responses.

OUTLINE. A carefully prepared structural pattern for a speech or case which clarifies the relationship of ideas in the message by placing information in a reasoned sequence and by indicating the coordinate and subordinate relationship of ideas.

PRIMA FACIE CASE. A case which establishes such a high degree of probability that the proposition would be accepted unless the case is refuted. It is usually established in the first affirmative constructive speech.

PROBE QUESTIONS. Cross-examination questions which require the respondent to defend or justify their reasons or use of data.

PROOF. Support for an idea or argument which the speaker offers in order to create belief in an audience. In debate, it consists of evidence and reasoning which is offered to the audience.

PROPOSITION. A judgment expressed in a declarative statement. In debate, it appears as an affirmative statement of the question to be resolved.

PROPOSITION OF FACT. A proposition which asserts that a fact is true or that an event took place.

PROPOSITION OF POLICY. A proposition which declares that a certain future action should be taken.

PROPOSITION OF VALUE. A proposition which does not call for a future action, but makes an evaluation or judgment.

QUOTE. A verb meaning to use words, sentences, or material from sources other than your own.

REASONING. The process of drawing inferences and conclusions from available information or data. In debate, it is the process of inferring relationships between evidence and assertions.

REBUTTAL. The process of defending arguments against attack. In debate, it is an additional speech allowed each speaker, following the constructive speeches, in which a speaker may attack the opponents' arguments in addition to defense, but may not introduce any new constructive arguments.

REFUTATION. The attempt to demonstrate the error or inadequacy of the opponents' case.

RESEARCH. The process of finding information and material to support ideas or arguments. It is most effective when conducted as the result of a carefully focused approach.

RESOLUTION. Used the same as proposition.

SIGN. A type of argument which asserts that the existence of fact A reliably indicates the existence of fact B.

STATUS QUO. Literally, "the state in which a thing is." In debate, it refers to the situation in existence as the debate begins.

STOCK ISSUE. A standard, or routine, issue which occurs in almost every debate.

TOPICALITY ISSUE. A basic issue in any debate which determines if the debate is actually concerned with the area stated by the proposition.

TOURNAMENT. The competitive gathering of speakers for various events, such as debate.

VALUE. A general statement of principles upon which one bases actions and beliefs.

WARRANT. The reasoning process by which we look at one bit of information (data) and decide what it means (claim).

Selected
Bibliography

This bibliography is by no means comprehensive but is intended to be a guide to references that are of special value in debate research. A complete guide to reference materials is the *Guide to Reference Books* edited by Eugene P. Sheehy (Chicago: American Library Association, 1976), with supplements.

Books About Debate

Brockriede, W., and Ehninger, D. *Decision by Debate*. 2d ed. New York: Harper and Row, 1978.

Church, R., and Willbanks, C. *Values and Policies in Controversy*. Scottsdale, AZ: Gorsuch Scarisbrick, 1986.

Freely, A. *Argumentation and Debate*. 5th ed. Belmont, CA: Wadsworth, 1981.

McBath, J., ed. *Forensics as Communication*. Skokie, IL: National Textbook Co., 1975.

Rieke, R., and Sillars, M. *Argumentation and the Decision Making Process*. 2d ed. New York: Wiley, 1982.

Swanson, D., and Zeuschner, R. *Participating in Intercollegiate Forensics*. Scottsdale, AZ: Gorsuch Scarisbrick, 1981.

Thomas, D. *Advanced Debate*. 2d ed. Skokie, IL: National Textbook Co., 1981.

Compiled Abstracts

Criminal Justice Abstracts
Criminology and Penology Abstracts
Environment Abstracts
International Political Abstracts
Psychological Abstracts
Resources in Education
Social Work and Research Abstracts
Sociological Abstracts

Indexes to Periodicals

Alternative Press Index
American History and Life
Business Periodicals Index
Consumers Index
Current Index to Journals in Education
Current Law Index
Education Index
Humanities Index
Index of Economics Articles
Index to Legal Periodicals
Index Medicus
Index to Periodical Articles Related to Law
International Index to Periodicals
Public Affairs Information Service Bulletin
Readers' Guide to Periodical Literature
Social Science Index

Indexes to Newspapers

Chicago Tribune Index
Index to The Christian Science Monitor
Index to the Los Angeles Times
New York Times Index

NewsBank
Official Washington Post Index
Wall Street Journal Index

Almanacs

Information Please Almanac
Whitaker's Almanack
World Almanac

Specialty Dictionaries

Ballentine's Law Dictionary
Black's Law Dictionary
Corpus Juris Secundum
Dictionary of Modern Economics
Dictionary of Philosophy
Dictionary of Politics
Encyclopedic Dictionary of Psychology
Words and Phrases

Specialty Compilations

The Annals (Political and Social Science)
American Statistical Index
Bulletin, The Public Affairs Information Service
Congressional Information Service
Congressional Quarterly Almanac
Congressional Quarterly Reports
Current History
Dictionary of American History
Dictionary of the History of Ideas
Editorials on File
Encyclopedia of American Foreign Affairs
Encyclopedia of Philosophy
Facts on File Yearbook: Weekly World New Digest

Keesling's Contemporary Archives
Labor Law Reporter
Monthly Catalog of U.S. Government Publications
National Journal
National Technical Information Service

Annuals

American Annual
Britannica Book of the Year
New International Yearbook
News Dictionary
Statesman's Year Book
Statistical Abstract of the United States

Microfilm, Electronic Based Sources

American Civilization History
Environfiche
ERIC (Education Resources Information Center)
HRAF (Human Relations Area File)
Statistical Reference Index

Guides to Bibliographies

A World Bibliography of Bibliographies
Bibliographic Index
United States Library of Congress Catalog

JON M. ERICSON is the dean of the School of Liberal Arts at California Polytechnic State University, San Luis Obispo, California. He has served as president of the Northern California Forensic Association (NCFA) and is a member of the forensics honor societies, Pi Kappa Delta and Delta Sigma Rho. He founded the American Issues debate tournaments on value questions while Director of Forensics at Stanford University.

JAMES J. MURPHY is professor of Rhetoric and Communication and faculty adviser to the Emil Mrak Forensic Union at the University of California, Davis. He was the founding president of the Northern California Forensic Association (NCFA) and has been Director of Forensics at Stanford University and faculty adviser to the Whig-Cliosophic forensics society at Princeton University.

RAYMOND BUD ZEUSCHNER is professor of Speech Communication and former Director of Forensics at California Polytechnic State University, San Luis Obispo, California. He is past president of the Cross Examination Debate Association (CEDA) and of the Northern California Forensic Association (NCFA) in addition to serving two terms as president of Phi Rho Pi, the National Junior College Speech Association.